AN

RELIGION

Theories, Traditions, & Ethics
LORA HOBBS • AUSTRA REINIS

Kendall Hunt
publishing company

Cover image © 2014 Shutterstock, Inc.

Kendall Hunt
publishing company

www.kendallhunt.com
Send all inquiries to:
4050 Westmark Drive
Dubuque, IA 52004-1840

Copyright © 2014 by Kendall Hunt Publishing Company

ISBN 978-1-4652-4698-1

All rights reserved. No part of this publication may be reproduced,
stored in a retrieval system, or transmitted, in any form or by any means,
electronic, mechanical, photocopying, recording, or otherwise,
without the prior written permission of the copyright owner.

Printed in the United States of America

Contents

Introduction v

An Introduction to Religion and the Study of Religion
Excerpts from William A. Young, *The World's Religions:
Worldviews and Contemporary Issues*
vii

Unit One: Theories of Religion   1
Religion as an Encounter with the Supernatural
Excerpts from Rudolf Otto, *The Idea of the Holy*
1

Religion as a Mind-Numbing Drug
Excerpts from Karl Marx, *Writings of the
Young Marx on Philosophy and Society*
10

Religion as a Wishful and Child-like Thinking
Excerpts from Sigmund Freud, *The Complete
Introductory Lectures on Psychoanalysis*
18

Religion as Ultimate Commitment
Excerpts from Paul Tillich, *The Dynamics of Faith*
28

Unit Two: Five Religious Traditions 39

Hinduism
41

Buddhism
44

Judaism
47

Christianity
50

Islam
53

Unit Three: Ethical Decision-Making 57

Love is the Supreme Law
Excerpts from Joseph Fletcher, *Situation Ethics: The New Morality*
60

Texts about WOMEN and about JIHAD in the QURAN
66

Ethics without Religion?
Excerpts from His Holiness the Dalai Lama, *Beyond Religion: Ethics for a Whole World*
Chapter 1, "Rethinking Secularism" and
Chapter 8, "Ethical Mindfulness in Everyday Life"
78

Introduction

Welcome to *An Introduction to Religion!* This reader is meant to introduce you to a variety of exciting aspects of the study of religion, as well as to lead you to ask some existential questions about your own approach to life. In today's globalized world, the knowledge you gain in studying religion will enhance your cultural competence, enabling you to understand and interact with people of faith traditions other than your own. Additionally, it will raise your awareness of how you, in current and/or future leadership roles, may approach ethical decision-making, as well as encourage you to be sensitive to the factors that influence how others make decisions.

Unit One deals with the deceptively simple question: What is religion? Religion is a commonplace phenomenon, but, as you will learn, scholars to date have not been able to formulate a definition that fits all forms of religion practiced by humans on the face of planet Earth. Instead, they have developed theories to explain the aspects of religion that each of them considered important from their particular areas of study. Some examples of these various perspectives on what religion is include: Is religion an experience of encounter with a supernatural power? Is it a deliberately chosen ultimate commitment? Or is it a mind-altering substance, or simply wishful thinking? Considering the theories of four famous thinkers may lead to you ask yourself: What is my experience of religion, if any? Who are my authorities when it comes to religion? And what does my religion, if I have one, do for me? By the way, one of the theorists would say that no matter who you are, even if you consider yourself an atheist, you DO have a religion!

Unit Two examines the history, beliefs, and traditional practices of five of the world's great religious traditions: Hinduism, Buddhism, Judaism, Christianity, and Islam. It invites you to explore Harvard University's "Pluralism Project" website where you will find basic information about each religion, as well as images and videos of various aspects of religious practice. In the course of learning about these religious traditions, you may find yourself asking: Are all religions basically the same? How have I come to believe what I believe? What leads others to believe differently? And what beliefs, if any, do various traditions share?

Unit Three introduces you to the varieties of ways in which human beings approach moral decisions, and explores some connections between ethical decision-making and religious belief. It considers questions such as: Can one be ethical without the influence of religion? Is there such a thing as morally evil behavior? Do I act on the basis of principles? If so, then what are my principles, and from where do they come? Or do I act on the basis of expected outcomes, and if so, what kinds of outcomes do I value?

So welcome again—to the exciting journey of self-understanding that lies ahead of you!

Lora Hobbs and Austra Reinis

An Introduction to Religion and the Study of Religion

Excerpts from William A. Young

The World's Religions: Worldviews and Contemporary Issues

© Marek Uliasz_Dreamstime.com

WHAT IS RELIGION?

The Problem of Defining Religion

One person joins the army of her country and enthusiastically kills enemy soldiers. Another refuses to become a soldier and spends time in prison for violating the compulsory service law of his country. One person dances

---

YOUNG, WILLIAM A., WORLD'S RELIGIONS, THE: WORLDVIEWS AND CONTEMPORARY ISSUES, 3rd, © 2010. Printed and Electronically reproduced by permission of Pearson Education, Inc., Upper Saddle River, New Jersey. (pp. 2–6, 12–17)

with abandon, holding poisonous snakes, gesticulating wildly. Another sits quietly for hours, seemingly frozen like a statue. One person talks about the earth as her mother and the birds, fish, and land animals as her sisters and brothers. Another speaks majestically of the human sovereignty over nature and implies that other animals are subordinate to humans. One person says that humankind's only hope is through faith in the mercy of the one and only God. Another asserts that many gods exist, but they are powerless to help humans reach the highest goal. Still another denies the existence of God or gods but seems to have an all-encompassing worldview that takes the place of faith in God or gods.

All of these seemingly contradictory behaviors and beliefs have been identified as "religious" by scholars in the field of religious studies, illustrating the difficulty of identifying the object of their study. If such diverse phenomena are "religious," is there any common denominator that enables us to distinguish religion from other human endeavors?

Scholars are frankly divided on this most basic question. Some argue that it is impossible to define religion in general (Smith 1991: 21). Any attempt to define religion as a whole inevitably falls victim, they say, to the bias of a particular religious or nonreligious point of view. Other scholars point out that "religion" is a Western term that has been imposed on other cultures (Hinnels 2005: 2, 283–84). Still others think that, given the basic diversity among religions, no single definition encompassing all religions is possible. Scholars of this perspective typically leave unaddressed the problem of defining religion.

Other interpreters, including the author of this text, think that a definition of religion in general is not only possible but essential to the study of religion (Smith 1998: 281–82). A definition may reflect the bias of its author, but readers have a right to know the basic perspective taken in a presentation on a subject, especially one as controversial as religion. If no suitable definition for religion can be found to guide the study, how will students know what they are studying *is* "religion"? Therefore, we will begin this study of the world's religions with a definition that we will use throughout our discussion.

Adopting a Working Definition of Religion

Many scholars have been sensitive to this problem and have developed what they call "functional" or "working" definitions of religion. A "functional" definition is one designed for a particular use, in this case the broad study of religion (Baird 1991). Such definitions are not intended to capture the *true* essence of religion, but rather intend only a framework for distinguishing and understanding religion. We will not attempt to review the many such definitions of religion proposed over the years. Typically, they have proven appropriate for the particular type of study to which they are related. There is no *one* right working definition of religion. From this perspective, each interpreter should stipulate and explain the definition adopted in his or her study.

The definition of religion developed for this examination of the world's religions is the following: Religion is human transformation in response to perceived ultimacy.

My task now is to convince you that this definition is appropriate and helpful for a study of the world's religions in an academic setting. To that end, we will first look at the three key words in the definition (*human, transformation,* and *ultimacy*) and then examine the definition as a whole.

Human The first decision one must make is whether to limit "religion" to humanity or to include other nonhuman life as religious creatures. Are dogs religious? What about plants? Our approach to this question is that if nonhuman beings *are* religious, we have not yet found a sufficiently open form of communication with them to be able to understand and describe their religions in an academic setting. Therefore, for the purposes of this study, we will stipulate that religion is a *human* phenomenon.

It should be noted that the definition leaves open the issue of whether religion is something humans engage in as individuals or groups. In fact, religion involves humans acting both by themselves and as communities, with some religions seeming to stress one over the other. A definition of religion adopted for a general study should not limit itself to either.

The inclusion of the term "human" in the definition also makes clear that religion is being understood as a *human* activity. This is important because some may wish to stipulate that the focus of activity in religion is "*God's* reaching out to humans." For the purposes of this study, religion is human behavior *in response to* some sort of perceived ultimacy such as God. This enables us to deal with what can be directly observed (that which humans say and do) rather than that which is beyond our direct observation (i.e., God).

Finally, the word *human* implies that, in any religion, the observer will find a particular understanding of what it means to be human. We tend to assume that there is one, self-evident view of the nature of humanity (which usually reflects our own particular religious perspective). In fact, we will find a diversity of teachings about the essential elements of "humanity." Do humans have "souls"? If so, are these souls unique? Do humans survive physical death? If so, how? Are humans fundamentally distinct from other living beings? As we study religions we must be sensitive to the diversity of understandings of "humanity" that we encounter.

Transformation Our definition emphasizes the dynamic quality of religion. Virtually every sort of human thought, feeling, or action *may* be religious. In order for anything human to qualify as religious, according to our definition, it must relate to a process of transformation, meaning *change* from one state of being to another. "Transformation" implies a situation prior to the change, the process of change itself, and the state that follows the change. Therefore, the single word *transformation* points us to three distinct aspects of religion.

First, religion identifies for individuals and/or groups a situation of life from which change is necessary. Such a state might be called the "problem" or "predicament" or, simply, "the human situation." One religion might identify "attachment to the material world" as this basic problem, another "an absence of harmony with the spirit world." We will maintain that a common feature of all religions is the explicit or implicit naming of a state *from* which transformation occurs.

Second, religion implies a state of existence that follows the process of transformation. This end may be expressed as an essentially individual phenomenon, as for example when a Buddhist monk experiences the blissful state called *nirvana* (see Chapter Four). Or it may be a communal situation, such as the new age that some branches of Judaism associate with their belief in the coming of a messiah (see Chapter Ten). The state may be said to occur for individuals before death, after death, or both. It may come as a result of perceived divine or human initiative. All that can be said in general is that religious transformation involves a "goal," an "ideal state" toward which the transformation is directed.

Third, religion involves a process, a "means" through which the transformation occurs. The "means of transformation" is at the heart of religion. The "means" typically involves identification with myths that tell the fundamental stories of the religion and the acting out of these myths in the form of rituals. In a religious context, language has transformative power. When invoked properly, or dramatically enacted by those entrusted with authority to do so, the "words of religion" enable people to participate in the process of change. As we shall see, in virtually all religions "myth and ritual" are present. We will spend more time later in this chapter discussing these terms since they have specialized meanings different (especially in the case of myth) from popular usage.

In addition to narratives and ritual acts, the "means" may also include direct experiences of that which inspires the transformation. The practice or belief in such direct experience is called *mysticism*. The transformation often entails the enactment of a right way of relating to others, the world, and one's self (ethics). The means may also involve assent to certain teachings and assertions (belief).

To reiterate a point made earlier, virtually any human activity may become part of the "means of transformation." In a real sense, the study of religion is the study of everything, because nothing can be ruled out *a priori* as nonreligious. And what is religious in one context may be considered nonreligious in another. In one setting, for example, killing an animal may be a matter of obtaining food, with no religious meaning. In other contexts, however, killing an animal may have deeply religious significance, either positive or negative. So, what *are* the criteria for distinguishing a religious phenomenon from other, nonreligious human endeavors?

Ultimacy There is a fairly broad consensus among scholars today that the critical factor in naming something "religious" is "ultimacy." Religious phenomena are those associated with that which a person or group perceives as ultimate in individual or communal life. "That which is ultimate" means whatever is at the focus of life, whatever defines what "life" or "true reality" is for a person or community. The ultimate is the center in the circle of life; it conditions and gives meaning to all of existence.

We commonly associate religion with an ultimacy that people experience or believe in as coming from a higher plane of existence than ordinary, earthly reality. We will call this type of perceived extraordinary reality "spiritual" or "supernatural," as opposed to the "material" or "natural" reality of the world directly accessible to the physical senses and interpreted by the rational mind. Indeed, most of the religions to be studied in this text are "spiritual" in their perception of ultimacy.

"Spiritual ultimacy" may be expressed in personal language, the imagery of "gods" and "goddesses." Those religions whose ultimacy is spiritual and personal speak of the ultimate as one or more gods or spirits. Christianity, for example, is such a religion, for its transformation is in response to an ultimacy perceived as a personal deity (see Chapter Eleven). Other religions may have a spiritual sense of ultimacy but view gods and spirits as either non-existent or at least not supreme. The Dao of Daoism, for example, although ultimate, is not a god (see Chapter Six).

The terminology that has developed in Western cultures to describe the various perceptions of spiritual ultimacies reflects a bias in favor of personal description. Belief in the existence of personal gods is called in general *theism*. Belief in the existence of one all-powerful god, to the exclusion of other gods, is called *monotheism*. The belief in the existence of a plurality of personal gods is called *polytheism*. The rejection of belief in personal gods (and by extension spiritual reality in general) is known as *atheism*. Less common examples of theistic belief are *henotheism* (many gods exist, but one is dominant) and *pantheism* (all reality is god) or pantheism (God is greater than but includes all reality).

However, not all perceptions of spiritual ultimacy use personal imagery. We will encounter a number of religions in which ultimacy is understood to be impersonal: a force, an energy, or a mysterious reality beyond our comprehension. For example, *monism* is the belief in an impersonal ultimacy that is characterized by absolute unity. From a monist perspective, the highest truth is the oneness of all reality. We will encounter monism in several religions, including Hinduism (see Chapter Three) and Daoism (see

Chapter Five).

The term *perceived* is used advisedly in this definition. It is present to clarify that the definition is not claiming to identify the *true* ultimacy, only that which different people have responded to as ultimate. A perceptive (no pun intended) reader might object that "perception" is an exercise of the human mind in relation to this world. How can one perceive that which is, by definition, beyond the realm of ordinary existence? In order to attempt to understand religions with spiritual ultimacies, we must be willing to assume for the purpose of the study the *possibility* of the perception of *spiritual* reality.

Secular Religions?

For most of human history, the vast majority of people have responded to what they perceive as spiritual ultimacy, whether personally or impersonally expressed. A characteristic of the modern world is the emergence of perceived ultimacies that are not spiritual but are of the physical or mental world we experience and express as humans. Some interpreters designate such systems as "ideologies" and distinguish them from religions, which they limit to movements that have a spiritual focus. However, because "spiritual" is not a necessary component of our definition, we may include such "secular ultimacies" in the scope of our study and identify them as "secular religions."

One of the most prevalent "secular religions" of the modern world has been Marxism, named after the nineteenth-century economic and social theorist Karl Marx (1818–1883). Marxists typically perceive ultimacy not as a god or some impersonal spiritual reality or force but as material reality understood in terms of the "laws" Karl

Marx described. Marxism identifies transformation of society from a state of "alienation," caused by economic oppression, to the communal utopia of the classless society (which would inevitably arise, Marxists believed, under the stewardship of the Communist Party). We will provide a fuller description of Marxism as a secular religion in Chapter Fourteen.

Marxism is perhaps the most famous "secular religion," but there are others, now more influential than Marxism, in the early part of the twenty-first century. Some would argue that *laissez-faire* capitalism is a secular religion that is now more threatening to spiritual religions than Marxism (Loy 2000). Under unrestrained capitalism, the pursuit of material wealth can become—for some—a pattern of ultimacy that drives out a meaningful sense of spirituality for individuals and societies. Capitalism is related to a popular secular perception of ultimacy some consider to be the fastest-growing religion in the contemporary world: *consumerism*.

Our contention is that the definition of religion as "human transformation in response to perceived ultimacy" provides a helpful framework for the objective study of the world's religions. It is inclusive enough to encompass the breadth of "spiritual" religions, as well as the "secular" religions we find in the modern world. But it is also narrow enough to provide a series of specific characteristics that enable us to distinguish religious from nonreligious phenomena.

HOW MIGHT RELIGION BE STUDIED?

There is no single accepted method in the academic study of religion. That should not be surprising, given the fact, as we have acknowledged, that there is no consensus on just what "religion" is, yet there is wide agreement that virtually any human activity or belief may fall at one time or another within the domain of religion. In fact, religious studies is by nature an interdisciplinary activity, drawing on the methods of a wide variety of academic disciplines. We will outline some of the approaches to the study of religion by dividing them in terms of the fundamental purpose of the study. Then we will clarify the way in which religion will be examined in this work. (For fuller discussions of the range of academic theories of religion and methods of studying religion, see Alles 2008; Cunningham and Kelsey 2001; Herling 2007; Hinnells 2005; Kunin 2003; Pals 2006; and Strenski 2006).

Evaluative Methods of Studying Religion

One way to distinguish methods in the study of religion is in terms of the purpose of the study: religion may be studied for the sake of *evaluation* or *description*. Sometimes the two are combined, but for the purposes of an introductory study, it is important to distinguish them. Those whose goal is evaluation are seeking to judge the truth of religion or religions. They want to know whether the claims of individual religions (or religion in general) have merit and seek to establish criteria for assessing them. Two common evaluative methods are the *religious* and the *philosophical.*

Religious As we have already acknowledged, any observer inevitably looks at other religions from the perspective of his or her own perception of ultimacy. In the "religious" method, however, the student has as a fundamental goal an assessment of the truth of other religions from one religion's point of view. For example, if I am a Zoroastrian, I might examine other religions to look for the degree to which they accord with truth as understood from a Zoroastrian perspective. The same approach may be taken with any religion as a starting point. Or I might start my study from the perspective that there is no truth to the claim that spiritual reality exists. I would then study religions with spiritual ultimacies in order to refute their teachings. Because I would hold as ultimate the assertion that there is no spiritual reality, this perspective would still fall under the heading of a "religious approach to religion" (using our definition of religion).

Philosophical Another method of studying religion with an evaluative goal is the *philosophy of religion*. Here, however, the truth claims of religions are assessed not from the perspective of a particular religion but from the standpoint of their susceptibility to being proven or disproven on the basis of rational argument. Does God (or any other spiritual ultimacy) exist? Is there life after death? Are there miracles? A philosopher of religion will carefully analyze each of the terms of these assertions to determine the degree to which they may be said to have any rational meaning and to have a basis in observable reality.

Descriptive Methods of Studying Religion

In contrast to evaluative methods of studying religion, a descriptive study of religion is designed not so much to make judgments about the truth of religion or religions as to understand religion and the roles religions play in human life. Those committed to describing religion typically suspend judgment on the question of the truth or falsity of that which they are studying, at least while they are engaged in descriptive study. Descriptive methods include the *phenomenological, historical, functional,* and *comparative.*

Phenomenological   Simply stated, the phenomenological approach to the study of religion attempts to understand religion from the perspective of religious persons themselves. Perhaps you have heard the popular saying, derived from a Native American proverb, that you should not judge a person until you have walked a mile in his or her moccasins. The phenomenological method, in the sense used here, holds that "understanding" should precede "evaluation" when it comes to studying religion. A primary goal of the initial phase of study, exponents of this method contend, should be to understand the phenomenon of religion as much as possible *sui generis* (i.e., on its own terms) rather than "reducing" religion to one of its various functions. In other words, when studying Islam, the goal should be to understand Islam emphatically—in other words, as Muslims do rather than as Islam is portrayed by others. That is an idealistic, perhaps utopian objective. How can we possibly perceive ultimacy as others do? In addition, Islam has various meanings in different historical and cultural contexts. The fact that we cannot fully attain the phenomenological goal does not mean that we should not try, advocates of this method argue. What is required is a willingness to consciously "bracket off" one's own assumptions about religion in general—and other religions in particular—long enough to see the world from another religious point of view. We must attempt to let religions "speak for themselves" and listen sensitively to what we hear. (For full discussions of the phenomenological method, including criticisms that it is more evaluative than descriptive, see Flood 1999; Hinnells 2005: 182–207; McCutcheon 1997; and Pals 2006: 193–228.)

Historical The historical approach seeks to understand religions as they have come into existence and developed through time. An historical study will typically examine the origins of a particular religion, its earliest expressions, its spread and oftentimes divisions, and its progress to the present.

Functional A functional study seeks to understand the function or role religion plays in a particular human context. Psychologists of religion typically study the function of religion in the makeup and development of individuals. Sociologists of religion examine the role religion plays in human groups, from the family to the entire society. Anthropologists of religion engage in a method of study functional in intent, but often phenomenological in spirit. They typically focus on the place of religion in the cultures of indigenous and other peoples, through a process of participation in and observation of the people of that culture. The common denominator in the functional approach is that the primary interest is in understanding the role of religion in the life of an individual, society, or culture. The functional approach overlaps with the evaluative when the question of whether religion is "functional" or "dysfunctional" in the various contexts is raised.

Comparative The comparative method seeks to understand religion by looking for that which is common among religions. Its basic question is whether there is an "essence" that all religions share. The method also focuses on fundamental patterns of religious expression. For example, a comparativist might find common meanings in the use of water in the rituals of various religions. (For full discussions of the comparative method, see Idinopulos, Wilson, and Hangues 2006; and Sharma 2005.)

HOW WILL WE STUDY THE WORLD'S RELIGIONS?

Our method of studying religions in this work will be fundamentally descriptive. Readers are urged, to the maximum degree possible, to put aside their own assumptions about the truth of religion or religions and seek to understand the variety of religions studied in this book on the religions' own terms. In other words, if you begin this study fervently believing in the truth claims of a particular religion, try hard not to assess other religions from your own religious perspective. Instead, resolve to try your best to understand what each religion means to its own adherents. Or, if you come to this study antagonistic toward religion (perhaps because of a negative experience with a particular religion), you are also encouraged to set aside your prior perspective. Simply coming to a basic understanding of the world's religions is hard enough; carrying one's own baggage along on the journey of discovery can make it much more difficult. Once you have achieved an understanding of the various religions of the world, you will be in a better and fairer position to make informed judgments about them, and your discussion of religions with others will be freer of the biases we so often carry into such dialogues.

Our descriptive study of the world's religions will be *historical, comparative,* and—above all—*phenomenological.* We will examine the origins and stages of development of each religion, and (after the indigenous religions) its written, sacred texts. From the perspective of phenomenological study, at the most basic level, religions order reality. In other words, each group of religions and each individual religion has a "worldview" rooted in its distinctive "perceptions of ultimacy." To appreciate this critically important dimension of religion, we have created a framework for understanding religious worldviews. At the outset of the discussion of each group of religions, and at the heart of our examination of each particular religion, we will typically apply this framework as a tool of analysis. In addition, the framework will provide a basis for descriptive (rather than evaluative) comparison of religions.

A Framework for Understanding and Comparing Religious Worldviews

The framework for understanding religious worldviews that we will employ is based on the definition of religion developed for this study: human transformation in response to perceived ultimacy. We have already begun to analyze the elements of this definition; it can be further expressed in terms of seven questions that may be asked of each religion in order to develop an understanding of its worldview. This framework will be useful in both understanding and comparing the religions we are studying.

What Does It Mean to Be Human?   Each religion has its own view of what constitutes human nature and the relationship between humans and other beings. If the religion is spiritual (rather than secular), humans are understood to have not only material, but also spiritual natures. For example, some spiritual religions claim that humans have individual souls, while others reject the notion of separate human souls. Religions also place humans in the world. For example, some religions are anthropocentric (human centered), claiming a unique spiritual identity for humans and a relationship of dominance over the rest of the world; others are biocentric (centered on all living beings together), rejecting the view that humans have special spiritual status or are superior to other forms of life. Still others might be called ecocentric (centered on all reality together), embracing the spiritual interconnectedness and ultimate identity of all life.

What Is the Basic Human Problem?   Each religion identifies a situation common to humanity, which results in the need for transformation. For example, some religions identify the fundamental human dilemma as entrapment in a cycle of birth, death, and rebirth. Others see the human problem as a lack of harmony with the rest of life. Still others see the problem as human separation or alienation from a personal god.

What Is the Cause of the Problem?   Religions include understandings of what is at the root of the basic human dilemma. Religions that see the problem as separation from a personal god often see the cause of human disobedience of the deity's will. By contrast, religions identifying the problem as being stuck in the cycle of rebirth tend to view human desire and ignorance of the spiritual as the causes. And religions stressing disharmony put the emphasis on human forgetfulness of the way of harmony.

What Is the End or Goal of Transformation? If religions identify a basic human problem and the cause of the dilemma, they also envision an ideal state for humans. We may call this state the end or goal of transformation. For example, religions in which the problem is entrapment in the cycle of rebirth claim that the ideal state is liberation from the cycle; typically, they are rich in imagery of the nature of the liberated existence. However, religions focusing on human disobedience of a personal god portray a state of existence in which humans are reconciled with the deity, typically enjoying a life beyond earthly existence.

What Are the Means of Transformation? At the heart of each religion are means that will enable the transformation to occur. For religions in which liberation from the cycle of rebirth is the end or goal, the means of transformation focus on the overcoming of material attachment and spiritual ignorance. However, if the end or goal is repairing the breach with a personal god caused by human disobedience, the means will involve reorientation to the way of life ordained by the deity. For religions in which the end or goal is harmony with all beings, the means typically are all-encompassing, involving every aspect of life.

What Is the Nature of Reality? If religions do indeed order reality, then it is important to understand how each religion constructs time and space. For example, for religions in which the issue is the cycle of birth, death, and rebirth, the understanding of time is obviously cyclical, with beginnings and endings of each cycle. By contrast, other religions understand time as moving from a beginning to a definitive end. Space is also understood from the perspective of the perceived ultimacy. For example, as we shall see in Chapter Two, indigenous religions are typically rooted in particular places and construct ordered space around a specific center.

What Is the Sacred, and How May the Sacred Be Known? In this study we use the term *sacred* as a synonym for the perceived ultimacy that distinguishes each religion. While it is common to think of the sacred as synonymous with the spiritual, that is not the case in our approach. Rather, that which is perceived as ultimate may be either spiritual or secular. The sacred may be the personal god or gods of a theistic religion or an impersonal energy or force. An important and related question is how the sacred may be made known. For example, for religions in which the problem is spiritual ignorance, the sacred is often made known through a disciplined pursuit of spiritual knowledge. However, monotheistic religions often claim that the only way the sacred may be known is through some act of self-revelation on the part of the god at the center of the religion, typically through the agency of a person or persons.

It may be useful for you at this point to consider your own responses to these seven questions. Do you find them difficult to answer, or do responses spring easily to mind? Regardless of your answer, as you study other religious worldviews, you will have the opportunity to reflect on your own. But remember, please place the priority on *understanding* other religions before you evaluate them!

Symbols, Myths, and Rituals

Because of their central importance to the academic study of religion, we must clarify three important, interrelated terms: *symbol, myth,* and *ritual* (see also Campbell 1988; Paden 1988 and 2003).

Symbols In general, a *symbol* is something that stands for something else. Drivers know that a red, octagonal sign at an intersection means "Stop!" The sign "symbolizes" the concept of "stopping" within the rules established for driving. Symbols may be objects, like the sign, or they may be gestures or sounds. When a baseball umpire raises his or her right hand, a strike is being called. When a movie director says "Cut!" the actors know that they should stop the scene. Religion is full of symbols in this general sense: objects, gestures, and sounds that reveal some aspect of whatever is ultimate in the religion. In Hinduism, for example, pictures of deities often show the god as having a number of arms as a visual way of expressing the power of the god. When a Jew says "*Shema' yisrael...*" ("Hear, O Israel..."), he or she is articulating a belief in the unity of the personal deity at the heart of Judaism.

However, many students of religion suggest a somewhat more specialized meaning for the term *symbol* when applying it to religion. More than simply representing something else, a religious "symbol" enables people to participate in that to which the symbol points. For example, when Hindus walk around (circumambulate) the object that symbolizes a particular deity, they are actually experiencing the sacred reality of that god. When a Roman Catholic priest lifts the "host" and says the prescribed words, the wafer is not a mere *representation* of the "body of Christ." When worshippers take the bread, they believe they are actually receiving Christ. Although religious people often disagree on the precise meaning of symbolic "participation," the belief that symbols (whether simple or elaborate) are essential to their contact with that which they deem ultimate is held in common. In studying a religion, awareness of the rich symbols that are present, and their particular usage, is critical to understanding.

Myths The dominant contemporary usage of the term *myth* is much different than its specialized meaning in the study of religion. In current general usage, myths are "false stories" because they conflict with what we know empirically to be true. For example, we might say that the belief that casual contact spreads the AIDS virus is a myth because scientific research has shown that to be untrue. To say in response to someone's story, "That's a myth!" is to denigrate the account, relegating it to the realm of the unbelievable.

In the academic study of religion, the term *myth* has a specialized meaning. In our study we will use "myth" for stories about whatever people perceive to be ultimate and which they therefore accept as *true* reality. Myths are often called "foundational stories" because they typically serve to create the basic patterns of order (cosmos) for those who believe them. They are paradigmatic, meaning that they reveal the way life is to be understood and lived by those who are grasped by the particular ultimacy with which the myth is concerned.

In the popular understanding, only "primitive" (and now discredited) religions had myths. They may be interesting to study (like the myths surrounding the Olympian gods), but they are now "dead." Contemporary students of religion typically take the position that *every* religion (whether spiritual or secular) has myths, for every religion has narratives about that which is ultimate—foundational stories that are at the heart of the religion.

One of the most common types of myths is the "myth of origins" (*cosmogonic myth*), which recounts the story of how that which is ultimate gave rise to all experienced reality. For Judaism and Christianity, for example, the first chapters of the Book of Genesis constitute a cosmos created by God. Virtually every religion has a myth of origins that fulfills a similar function. One of the fruitful ways to compare religions is to examine the cosmogonic myths popular in the religions.

Other myths relate to that toward which ordinary time is moving, rather than that from which it comes. They are called *eschatological myths*, and they are particularly common in the religions that hold a linear view of time. For example, the Christian Bible ends with a book that tells the myth of the "end time." As in the Book of Revelation, most end-time myths tell of how the order present in the time of origins will be completely restored at the end of time. Religions that take a cyclical view of time, like Hinduism, still have mythic accounts of the end of the current age, which will be destroyed before the next cosmic cycle begins.

Because they "stand outside ordinary time," myths speak of a time that is eternally present and repeatable (Eliade 1959: 68–113). That is, if the story of the myth is not limited to a particular time, then it is equally true and real at the particular moment at which it is told. The telling of a myth relates not so much to something that happened within time (although myths may relate to historical events), but draws the eternal into the present reality. For example, for Jewish people the story of the deliverance of the people of ancient Israel from slavery in Egypt (told in the Book of Exodus in the Hebrew Bible) is a "foundational story," or myth. Although the story of the deliverance presumably occurred in some form within time, the story about these events is a "myth," which speaks of how God interacts with his people at all times. When the story is recounted, those who accept it as "myth" experience it not only as an account of what "happened" but what continually "happens."

One of the critical steps in the study of any religion, spiritual or secular, is to ask, "What are its myths?" Myths are not confined to religions with spiritual ultimacies. So-called secular religions have "foundational stories" that order the cosmos they inhabit and eschatological stories that reveal that toward which time is moving. For example, Marxism constructs a narrative of historical events to show how the phenomenon of class struggle keeps repeating itself. It also envisions the "classless society" that will represent the culmination of ordinary, class-conscious history. The vibrancy of a religion can be measured in part by the power of the religion's myths to continue to lay the foundations for ordered reality for the people who tell them. Living myths are not only stories told but realities lived. They provide the models for living, for groups as a whole as well as for individuals.

Rituals Another term important in the study of religion in general is *ritual*. If myths are stories outside time and space, which order reality for those who accept them as true, then "rituals" are those actions within time and space that bring the power of myth into the lives of the people who practice them. Ritual is symbolic action that enables persons to participate in transformation in response to ultimacy. The source of ritual is myth. Rituals are often, one might say, "myths enacted." Myths express their order in word and image; rituals dramatize the ordering to the cosmos in terms of performance. For example, if the story of the deliverance of Egypt (Exodus 12–15) is a basic Jewish myth, then the Passover celebration is the ritual through which the myth is enacted, and through which the people may participate in the transformation in response to the ultimacy perceived in the myth. Through participation in the ritual, the individual or community steps outside ordinary time and space and enters, during the ritual, into sacred, "ordered" time and space.

Rituals create "sacred space," areas set apart or distinguished (temporarily or permanently) from ordinary usage to become arenas for the experience of the ultimate. Whether the context is a magnificent cathedral or a small home shrine, it is the conducting of rituals that transforms these spaces into "true space," where encounters with ultimacy order and give meaning to life.

Rituals order time, creating "moments" amid ordinary time into which the sacred enters to create cosmos. Some ritual observances are recurrent, creating a calendar for those who share the same perception of ultimacy. For example, in traditional Christian cultures, the year is ordered according to the series of festivals that enact the Christian myth (such as Easter and Christmas). "The periodicity of ritual time . . . ensures the perpetual grounding of world in its myth. Through daily, weekly, monthly, or annual ritual time, myth is recoverable." (Paden 1988: 101). In most religions there are "great" festivals that order the entire year at the time of transition from one year to another. Typically, there is a time of purification involving restriction and denial, followed by a time of celebration and rebirth. For example, the Christian "new year" is created by the sequence of the purificatory period called Lent, climaxing in death on Good Friday, followed by the time of rebirth at Easter.

In addition, there are other festivals of renewal on a monthly, weekly, or daily basis. In many indigenous religions, and in traditional practice in other religions, all of time is sacralized through the daily repetition of rituals.

Periodic rituals are for groups and also for individuals. In most religions, individuals celebrate their birthday, their marriage day, or the death of a family member as recurrent times of renewal. For the times of transition in the life of the individual (birth, adulthood, marriage, death), there are "rites of passage," to mark as well as order these moments.

Today, rituals are often dismissed as a "waste of time" by those for whom the associated myths have no power. However, look at your own life or the lives of others and ask yourself if you and they do not have certain "rituals" that order life? For some people in modern, materialistic society the "weekend" is ritual time, with the Friday or Saturday night "party" serving as a focus and frame for the experience of "true reality." At the party they "step outside ordinary time" and enter into a transformed reality that creates a sense (at least temporarily) of meaningfulness for an otherwise rather meaningless existence.

Terms for Study and Discussion

1. atheism
2. comparative method
3. cosmogonic myth
4. descriptive approach
5. eschatological myth
6. evaluative approach
7. monotheism
8. myth
9. periodic rituals
10. phenomenological method
11. philosophy of religion
12. polytheism
13. religion
14. rites of passage
15. rituals
16. secular religion
17. symbol
18. theism

UNIT ONE:
Theories of Religion

Religion as an Encounter with the Supernatural

Rudolf Otto (1869–1937) was fascinated by the mystical and experiential dimensions of religion. He was born in northern Germany near the city of Hanover, an area of Germany where the state religion was a form of Protestant Christianity. Wanting to become a Lutheran minister, Otto studied Lutheran theology at the universities of Erlangen and Göttingen and wrote his dissertation on Martin Luther's understanding of the Holy Spirit. When he finished his studies, the church authorities decided his views were too liberal for him to be a good candidate for the ministry, so Otto decided to pursue an academic career. He served as professor at the Universities of Breslau (1915–1917) and Marburg (1917–1937).

Otto was interested not only in Christianity, but in other religions as well. From 1911 to 1912, with funding from the German government, Otto undertook a "world tour" that took him to India, Burma, China, Japan, Egypt, and Jerusalem, where he learned about and experienced many religions, including Hinduism, Buddhism, Islam, and Judaism. He asked himself, "What is it that all religions have in common?" and answered this question in his most famous book, *The Idea of the Holy*, which he published in 1917.

Excerpts from Rudolf Otto

The Idea of the Holy

© Marilyn Volan_Dreamstime.com

CHAPTER II

'NUMEN' AND THE 'NUMINOUS'

'Holiness'—'the holy'—is a category of interpretation and valuation peculiar to the sphere of religion. It is, indeed, supplied by transference to another sphere—that of ethics—but it is not itself derived from this. While it is complex, it contains a quite specific element or 'moment', which sets it apart from 'the rational' in the meaning we gave to that word above, and which remains inexpressible…in the sense that it completely eludes apprehension in terms of concepts. The same thing is true (to take a quite different region of experience) of the category of the beautiful.

IDEA OF THE HOLY translated by Harvey (1958) pp. 5–10, 12–13.
By permission of Oxford University Press.

Now these statements would be untrue from the outset if 'the holy' were merely what is meant by the word, not only in common parlance, but in philosophical, and generally even in theological usage. The fact is we have come to use the words 'holy', 'sacred' in an entirely derivative sense, quite different from that which they originally bore. We generally take 'holy' as meaning 'completely good'; it is the absolute moral attribute, denoting the consummation of moral goodness. In this sense Kant calls the will which remains unwaveringly obedient to the moral law from the motive of duty a 'holy' will; here clearly we have simply the *perfectly moral* will. In the same way we may speak of the holiness or sanctity of duty or law, meaning merely that they are imperative upon conduct and universally obligatory.

But this common usage of the term is inaccurate. It is true that all this moral significance is contained in the word 'holy', but it includes in addition—as even we cannot but feel—a clear overplus of meaning, and this it is now our task to isolate…

Accordingly, it is worthwhile, as we have said, to find a word to stand for this element in isolation, this 'extra' in the meaning of 'holy' above and beyond the meaning of goodness. By means of a special term we shall the better be able, first, to keep the meaning clearly apart and distinct, and second, to apprehend and classify connectedly whatever subordinate forms or stages of development it may show. For this purpose I adopt a word coined from the Latin *numen*. *Omen* has given us 'ominous' and there is no reason why from *numen* we should not similarly form a word 'numinous'. I shall speak, then, of a unique 'numinous' category of value and of a definitely 'numinous' state of mind, which is always found wherever the category is applied.

CHAPTER III

THE ELEMENTS IN THE 'NUMINOUS'

Creature-Feeling

The reader is invited to direct his mind to a moment of deeply-felt religious experience, as little as possible qualified by other forms of consciousness. Whoever cannot do this, whoever knows no such moments in his experience, is requested to read no farther; for it is not easy to discuss questions of religious psychology with one who can recollect the emotions of his adolescence, the discomforts of indigestion, or, say, social feelings, but cannot recall any intrinsically religious feelings. We do not blame such a one, when he tries for himself to advance as far as he can with the help of such principles of explanation as he knows, interpreting 'aesthetic' in terms of sensuous pleasure, and 'religion' as a function of the gregarious instinct and social standards, or as something more primitive still. But the artist, who for his part has an intimate personal knowledge of the distinctive element in the aesthetic experience, will decline his theories with thanks, and the religious man will reject them even more uncompromisingly.

Next, in the probing and analysis of such states of the soul as that of solemn worship, it will be well if regard be paid to what is unique in them rather than to what they have in common with similar states. To be *rapt* in worship is one thing; to be morally *uplifted* by the contemplation of a good deed is another; and it is not to their common features, but to those elements of emotional content peculiar to the first that we would have attention directed as precisely as possible. As Christians we undoubtedly here first meet with feelings familiar enough in a weaker form in other departments of experience, such as feelings of gratitude, trust, love, reliance, humble submission, and dedication. But this does not by any means exhaust the content of religious worship. Not in any of these have we got the special features of the quite unique and incomparable experience of solemn worship. In what does this consist?

Schleiermacher has the credit of isolating a very important element in such an experience. This is the 'feeling of dependence'. But this important discovery of Schleiermacher is open to criticism in more than one respect.

In the first place, the feeling or emotion with which he really has in mind in this phrase is in its specific quality not a 'feeling of dependence' in the 'natural' sense of the word. As such, other domains of life and other regions of experience than the religious occasion the feeling, as a sense of personal insufficiency and impotence, a consciousness of being determined by circumstances and environment. The feeling of which Schleiermacher wrote has an undeniable analogy with these states of mind: they serve as an indication to it, and its nature may be elucidated by them, so that, by following the direction in which they point, the feeling itself may be spontaneously felt. But the feeling is at the same time also qualitatively different from such analogous states of mind. Schleiermacher himself, in a way, recognizes this by distinguishing the feeling of pious or religious dependence from all other feelings of dependence. His mistake is in making the distinction merely that between 'absolute' and 'relative' dependence, and therefore a difference of degree and not of intrinsic quality. What he overlooks is that, in giving the feeling the name 'feeling of dependence' at all, we are really employing what is no more than a very close analogy. Anyone who compares and contrasts the two states of mind introspectively will find out, I think, what I mean. It cannot be expressed by means of anything else, just because it is so primary and elementary a datum in our physical life, and therefore only definable through itself. It may perhaps help him if I cite a well-known example, in which the precise 'moment' or element of religious feeling of which we are speaking is most actively present. When Abraham ventures to plead with God for the men of Sodom, he says (Gen. xviii.27): 'Behold now, I have taken upon me to speak unto the Lord, which am but dust and ashes.' There you have a self-confessed 'feeling of dependence', which is yet at the same time far more than, and something other than, *merely* a feeling of dependence. Desiring to give it a name of its own, I propose to call it 'creature-consciousness' or creature-feeling. It is the emotion of a creature, submerged and overwhelmed by its own nothingness in contrast to that which is supreme above all creatures.

It is seen that, once again, this phrase, whatever it is, is not a *conceptual* explanation of the matter. All that this new term, 'creature-feeling', can express, is the note of submergence into nothingness before an overpowering, absolute might of some kind: whereas everything turns upon the *character* of this overpowering might, a character which cannot be expressed verbally, and can only be suggested indirectly through the tone and content of a man's feeling-response to it. And this response must be directly experienced in oneself to be understood.

CHAPTER IV

'MYSTERIUM TREMENDUM'

The Analysis of 'Tremendum'

We said above that the nature of the numinous can only be suggested by means of the special way in which it's reflected in the mind in terms of feeling. 'Its nature is such that it grips or stirs the human mind with this and that determinate affective state.' We have now to attempt to give a further indication of these determinate states. We must once again endeavor, by adducing feelings akin to them for the purpose of analogy or contrast, and by the use of metaphor and symbolic expressions, to make the states of mind we are investigating ring out, as it were, of themselves.

Let us consider the deepest and most fundamental elements in all strong and sincerely felt religious emotion. Faith unto salvation, trust, love—all these are there. But over and above these is an element which may also on occasion, quite apart from them, profoundly affect us and occupy the mind with a wellnigh bewildering strength. Let us follow it up with every effort of sympathy and imaginative intuition wherever it is to be found, in the lives of those around us, in sudden, strong ebullitions of personal piety and the frames of mind such ebullitions evince, in the fixed and ordered solemnities of rites and liturgies, and again in the atmosphere that clings to old religious monuments and buildings, to temples and to churches. If we do so we shall find we are dealing with something for which there is only one appropriate expression, '*mysterium tremendum*'. The feeling of it may at times come sweeping like a gentle tide, pervading the mind with a tranquil mood of deepest worship. It may pass over into a more set and lasting attitude of the soul, continuing, as it were thrillingly vibrant and resonant, until at last it dies away and the soul resumes its 'profane', non-religious mood of everyday experience. It may burst in sudden eruption up from the depths of the soul with spasms and convulsions, or lead to the strangest excitements, to intoxicated frenzy, to transport, and to ecstasy. It has its wild and demonic forms and can sink to an almost grisly horror and shuddering. It has its crude, barbaric antecedents and early manifestations, and again it may be developed into something beautiful and pure and glorious. It may become the hushed, trembling, and speechless humility of the creature in the presence of—whom or what? In the presence of that which is a *mystery* inexpressible and above all creatures.

It is again evident at once that here too our attempted formulation by means of a concept is once more a merely negative one. Conceptually *mysterium* denotes merely that which is hidden and esoteric, that which is beyond conception or understanding, extraordinary and unfamiliar. The term does not define the object more positively in its qualitative character. But though what is enunciated in the word is negative, what is meant is something absolutely and intensely positive. This pure positive we can experience in feelings, feelings which our discussion can help to make clear to us, in so far as it arouses them actually in our hearts.

Study and Critical-Thinking Questions

1. When we think of the word "holy," what does Otto assert that we think of? What does he say "holy" means (and does not mean)?
2. What does Otto mean by "numinous experience"? Can you think of times when you've had such an experience?
3. What is the "mysterium treme dum"? And what does it feel like?
4. When and where can the mysterium tremendum be found?
5. What is the relationship between a numinous experience and the mysterium tremendum?
6. According to Otto, what is religion? What is his theory of religion?

Questions for Class Discussion

1. What kind of definition (theory) of religion is Otto offering? Is it evaluative (religious or philosophical)? Is it descriptive (phenomenological, historical, functional, or comparative)? Why do you think so? (To be able to respond to this question, you may want to refer back to the previous piece written by William Young on the study of religion.)
2. What merits would you give to Otto's theory of religion?
3. What are some shortcomings with this theory?
4. How might you illustrate or diagram Otto's theory of religion?

Religion as a Mind-Numbing Drug

Karl Marx (1818–1883) was interested in the interconnections he perceived between religion, politics, and economics. He was born in the city of Trier in France. His family had Jewish origins: Both his grandfather and his uncle on his father's side had been rabbis in Trier, and there had been rabbis in his mother's family as well. Before Marx's birth, however, Marx's father had made a career-based decision to convert to Protestantism. Trier had come under German rule, Protestantism had become the new state religion, and Jews had begun to face a variety of discriminatory laws.

Marx studied law at the Universities of Bonn and Berlin. It was the time of the Industrial Revolution in Europe. Peasants were leaving their farms in the countryside in order to take jobs in factories. Because these jobs paid poorly, and dangerous working conditions led to injuries, workers and their children were often reduced to begging in the streets to feed themselves. Likely because of the poverty Marx saw on the streets, and because of the religious discrimination his own family had experienced, Marx began to write newspaper articles in which he denounced the oppressive and dehumanizing social order he felt the state and the church had jointly created. Marx's views on religion are most clearly expressed in an article he published in 1844 entitled "Introduction to a Critique of Hegel's Philosophy of Right."

Excerpts from Karl Marx

Writings of the Young Marx on Philosophy and Society

© 2014 Axel Lauer. Used under license from Shutterstock, Inc.

TOWARD THE CRITIQUE OF HEGEL'S PHILOSOPHY OF LAW: INTRODUCTION

For Germany the *criticism of religion* has been essentially completed, and criticism of religion is the premise of all criticism.

The *profane* existence of error is compromised when its *heavenly oratio pro aris et focis* [defense of altar and hearth] has been refuted. Man, who has found only the *reflection* of himself in the fantastic reality of heaven where he sought a supernatural being, will no longer be inclined to find the *semblance* of himself, only the non-human being, where he seeks and must seek his true reality.

Marx, *Writings of the Young Marx on Philosophy and Society*, translated by Loyd D. Easton and Kurt H. Guddar (Hackett 1997). Reprinted by permission of Hackett Publishing Company, Inc. All rights reserved. (pp. 249–251, 257–258, 262–264)

The basis of irreligious criticism is: *Man makes religion,* religion does not make man. And indeed religion is the self-consciousness and self-regard of man who has either not yet found or has already lost himself. But *man* is not an abstract being squatting outside the world. Man is the *world of men,* the state, society. This state and this society produce religion, which is an *inverted consciousness of the world* because they are an *inverted world.* Religion is the generalized theory of this world, its encyclopaedic compendium, its logic in popular form, its spiritualistic point d'honneur, its enthusiasm, its moral sanction, its solemn complement, its general ground of consolation and justification. It is the *fantastic realization* of the human essence inasmuch as the *human essence* possesses no true reality. The struggle against religion is therefore indirectly the struggle against *that world* whose spiritual *aroma* is religion.

Religious suffering is the *expression* of real suffering and at the same time the *protest* against real suffering. Religion is the sigh of the oppressed creature, the heart of a heartless world, as it is the spirit of spiritless conditions. It is the *opium* of the people.

The abolition of religion as people's *illusory* happiness is the demand for their *real* happiness. The demand to abandon illusions about their condition is a *demand to abandon a condition which requires illusions.* The criticism of religion is thus in *embryo a criticism of the vale of tears* whose *halo* is religion.

Criticism has plucked imaginary flowers from the chain, not so that man will wear the chain that is without fantasy or consolation but so that he will throw it off and pluck the living flower. The criticism of religion disillusions man so that he thinks, acts, and shapes his reality like a disillusioned man who has come to his senses, so that he revolves around himself and thus around his true sun. Religion is only the illusory sun that revolves around man so long as he does not revolve about himself.

Thus it is the *task of history*, once the *otherworldly truth* has disappeared, to establish the *truth of this world*. The immediate *task of philosophy* which is in the service of history is to unmask human self-alienation in its *unholy forms* now that it has been unmasked in its *holy form*. Thus the criticism of heaven turns into the criticism of the earth, the *criticism of religion* into the *criticism of law*, and the *criticism of theology* into the *criticism of politics*…

The clear proof of the radicalism of German theory and hence of its political energy is that it proceeds from the decisive *positive* transcendence of religion. The criticism of religion ends with the doctrine that man is *the highest being for man*, hence with the *categorical imperative to overthrow all conditions* in which is a degraded, enslaved, neglected, contemptible being—conditions that cannot better be described than by the explanation of a Frenchman on the occasion of a proposed dog tax: Poor dogs! They want to treat you like human beings!

Even historically, theoretical emancipation has a specific practical significance for Germany. For Germany's *revolutionary* past is theoretical—it is the *Reformation*. As the revolution then began in the brain of the *monk*, now it begins in the brain of the *philosopher*.

Luther, to be sure, overcame bondage based on *devotion* by replacing it with bondage based on *conviction*. He shattered faith in authority by restoring the authority of faith. He turned priests into laymen by turning laymen into priests. He freed man from outward religiosity by making religiosity the inwardness of man. He emancipated the body from its chains by putting chains on the heart.

But if Protestantism was not the true solution, it was the true formulation of the problem. The question was no longer the struggle of the layman against the *priest external to him* but of his struggle against *his own inner priest,* his *priestly nature.* And if the Protestant transformation of German laymen into priests emancipated the lay popes—the *princes* with their clerical set, the privileged and the Philistines—the philosophical transformation of priestly Germans into men will emancipate the *people.* But little as emancipation stops with princes, just as little will *secularization* of property stop with the *confiscation of church property* set in motion chiefly by hypocritical Prussia. At that time the Peasants' War, the most radical fact of German history, came to grief because of theology. Today, when theology itself has come to grief, the most unfree fact of German history—our *status quo*—will be shattered by philosophy.

Where, then, is the *positive* possibility of German emancipation?

Answer: In the formation of a class with *radical chains*, a class in civil society that is not of civil society, a class that is the dissolution of all classes, a sphere of society having a universal character because of its universal suffering and claiming no *particular* right because no *particular wrong* but *unqualified wrong* is perpetrated on it; a sphere that can invoke no *traditional* title but only a *human* title, which does not partially oppose the consequences but totally opposes the premises of the German political system; a sphere, finally, that cannot emancipate itself without emancipating itself from all the other spheres of society, thereby emancipating them; a sphere, in short, that is the *complete loss* of humanity and can only redeem itself through the *total redemption of humanity*. This dissolution of society as a particular class is the *proletariat*.

The proletariat is only beginning to appear in Germany as a result of the rising *industrial* movement. For it is not poverty from *natural circumstances* but *artificially produced* poverty, not the human masses mechanically oppressed by the weight of society but the masses resulting from the *acute disintegration* of society, and particularly of the middle class, which gives rise to the proletariat— though also, needless to say, poverty from natural circumstances and Christian-Germanic serfdom gradually join the proletariat.

Heralding the *dissolution of the existing order of things*, the proletariat merely announces the *secret of its own existence* because it *is* the *real* dissolution of this order. Demanding the *negation of private property*, the proletariat merely raises to the *principle of society* what society has raised to the principle *of the proletariat*, what the proletariat already embodies as the negative result of society without its action. The proletarian thus has the same right in the emerging order of things as the *German king* has in the existing order when he calls the people *his* people or a horse *his* horse. Declaring the people to be his private property, the king merely proclaims that the private owner is king.

As philosophy finds its *material* weapons in the proletariat, the proletariat finds it *intellectual* weapons in philosophy. And once the lightning of thought has deeply struck this unsophisticated soil of the people, the *Germans* will emancipate themselves to become *men*.

Let us summarize the result:

The only emancipation of Germany possible *in practice* is emancipation based on the theory proclaiming that man is the highest essence of man. In Germany emancipation from the *Middle Ages* is possible only as emancipation at the same time from *partial* victories over the Middles Ages. In Germany *no* brand of bondage can be broken without *every* brand of bondage being broken. Always seeking *fundamentals*, Germany can only make a *fundamental* revolution. The *emancipation of the German* is the *emancipation of mankind*. The *head* of this emancipation is *philosophy*, its *heart* is the *proletariat*. Philosophy cannot be actualized without the transcendence [*Aufhebung*] of the proletariat, the proletariat cannot be transcended without the actualization of philosophy.

Study and Critical-Thinking Questions

1. According to Marx, where does religion come from?
2. What does he say about the existence of God? Where did "God" come from according to Marx?
3. According to Marx, what is religion? (Simply write down some of Marx's phrases.)

4. According to Marx, in what ways do religious people (i.e., the proletariat, the factory workers) see religion as a source of comfort?
5. According to Marx, in what ways and by whom is religion used as a justification for oppression?
6. What does Marx say are some problems with religion?
7. What does he suggest as a better alternative than relying on God and religion?

Questions for Class Discussion

1. What kind of definition (theory) of religion is Marx offering? Is it evaluative (religious or philosophical)? Is it descriptive (phenomenological, historical, functional, or comparative)? Why do you think so? (To be able to respond to this question, you may want to refer back to the piece written by William Young on the study of religion.)
2. What merits would you give to Marx's theory of religion?
3. What are some shortcomings with this theory?
4. How might you illustrate or diagram Marx's theory of religion?

Religion as a Wishful and Child-like Thinking

Sigmund Freud (1856–1939), the father of modern psychology, identified what he thought was a relationship between religion and mental illness. He was born into a Jewish family in Freiberg, Moravia (now Pribor in the Czech Republic). When he was four years old, his family moved to Vienna in Austria. Freud studied medicine at the University of Vienna, graduating in 1881. The state religion in Austria was Catholic Christianity, and Freud experienced discrimination against himself as a Jew in medical school. Partly because of that, he decided to enter the field of psychiatry, to which he made substantial contributions over the course of his career. When the National Socialist Party (Nazis) came to power in Austria, Freud was persecuted for his ideas. He fled to London, where he soon died.

Freud's psychoanalytic theory was not only a theory of the personality or a method of healing. It was also a theory of culture and religion. Freud expressed his views on religion in a variety of works, including his *Introductory Lectures on Psychoanalysis* (1916–17) and *The Future of an Illusion* (1927). He argued that his psychoanalytic method had proven beyond a doubt that religion was simply a system of ideas and symbols that humanity had created in order to feel important and special in the world.

Excerpts from Sigmund Freud

The Complete Introductory Lectures on Psychoanalysis

© 2014 catwalker. Used under license from Shutterstock, Inc.

If we are to give an account of the grandiose nature of religion, we must bear in mind what it undertakes to do for human beings. It gives them information about the origin and coming into existence of the universe, it assures them of its protection and of ultimate happiness in the ups and downs of life and it directs their thoughts and actions by precepts which it lays down with its whole authority. Thus it fulfils three functions. With the first of them it satisfies the human thirst for knowledge; it does the same thing that science attempts to do with *its* means, and at that point enters into rivalry with it. It is to its second function

From NEW INTRODUCTORY LECTURES ON PSYCHO-ANALYSIS by Sigmund Freud, translated by James Strachey. Copyright © 1965, 1964 by James Strachey. Used by permission of W. W. Norton & Company, Inc. (pp. 625–628, 630–632)

that it no doubt owes the greatest part of its influence. Science can be no match for it when it soothes the fear that men feel of the dangers and vicissitudes of life, when it assures them of a happy ending and offers them comfort in unhappiness. It is true that science can teach us how to avoid certain dangers and that there are some sufferings which it can successfully combat; it would be most unjust to deny that it is a powerful helper to men; but there are many situations in which it must leave a man to his suffering and can only advise him to submit to it. In its third function, in which it issues precepts and lays down prohibitions and restrictions, religion is furthest away from science. For science is content to investigate and to establish facts though it is true that from its applications rules and advice are derived on the conduct of life. In some circumstances these are the same as those offered by religion, but, when this is so, the reasons for them are different.

The convergence between these three aspects of religion is not entirely clear. What has an explanation of the origin of the universe to do with the inculcation of certain particular ethical precepts? The assurances of protection and happiness are more intimately linked with the ethical requirements. They are the reward for fulfilling these commands; only those who obey them may count upon these benefits, punishment awaits the disobedient. Incidentally, something similar is true of science. Those who disregard its lessons, so it tells us, expose themselves to injury.

The remarkable combination in religion of instruction, consolation and requirements can only be understood if it is subjected to a genetic analysis. This may be approached from the most striking point of the aggregate, from its instruction on the origin of the universe; for why, we may ask, should a cosmogony be a regular component of religious systems? The doctrine is, then, that the universe was created by a being resembling a man, but magnified in every respect, in power, wisdom, and the strength of his passions—an idealized super-man. Animals as creators of the universe point to the influence of totemism, upon which we shall have a few words at least to say presently. It is an interesting fact that this creator is always only a single being, even when there are believed to be many gods. It is interesting, too, that the creator is usually a man, though there is far from being a lack of indications of female deities; and some mythologies actually make the creation begin with a male god getting rid of a female deity,[1] who is degraded into being a monster. Here the most interesting problems of detail open out; but we must hurry on. Our further path is made easy to recognize, for this god-creator is undisguisedly called 'father'. Psycho-analysis infers that he really is the father, with all the magnificence in which he once appeared to the small child. A religious man pictures the creation of the universe just as he pictures his own origin.

This being so, it is easy to explain how it is that consoling assurances and strict ethical demands are combined with a cosmogony. For the same person to whom the child owed his existence, the father (or more correctly, no doubt, the parental agency compounded of the father and mother), also protected and watched over him in his feeble and helpless state, exposed as he was to all the

---

1. [Freud had considerably more to say about female deities in Essay III, Park I, Section D, of *Moses and Monotheism* (1939a).]

dangers lying in wait in the external world; under his father's protection he felt safe. When a human being has himself grown up, he knows, to be sure, that he is in possession of greater strength, but his insight into the perils of life has also grown greater, and he rightly concludes that fundamentally he still remains just as helpless and unprotected as he was in his childhood, that faced by the world he is still a child. Even now, therefore, he cannot do without the protection which he enjoyed as a child. But he has long since recognized, too, that his father is a being of narrowly restricted power, and not equipped with every excellence. He therefore harks back to the mnemic image of the father whom in his childhood he so greatly overvalued. He exalts the image into a deity and makes it into something contemporary and real. The effective strength of his mnemic image and the persistence of his need for protection jointly sustain his belief in God.

The third main item in the religious programme, the ethical demand, also fits into this childhood situation with ease. I may remind you of Kant's famous pronouncement in which he names, in a single breath, the starry heavens and the moral law with us [see p. 61 above].[2] However strange this juxtaposition may sound—for what have the heavenly bodies to do with the question of whether one human creature loves another or kills him?—it nevertheless touches on a great psychological truth. The same father (or parental agency) which gave the child life and guarded

---

2. [In the original edition the present sentence read: 'In a famous pronouncement the philosopher Kant named the existence of the starry heavens and that of the moral law within us as the most powerful witnesses to the greatness of God.' It was changed to the form translated above in G.S. (1934)—the earlier quotation of the same passage having no doubt been previously overlooked.]

him against its perils, taught him as well what he might do and what he must leave undone, instructed him that he must adapt himself to certain restrictions on his instinctual wishes, and made him understand what regard he was expected to have for his parents and brothers and sisters, if he wanted to become a tolerated and welcome member of the family circle and later on of larger associations. The child is brought up to a knowledge of his social duties by a system of loving rewards and punishments, he is taught that his security in life depends on his parents (and afterwards other people) loving him and on their being able to believe that he loves them. All these relations are afterwards introduced by men unaltered into their religion. Their parents' prohibitions and demands persist within them as a moral conscience. With the help of this same system of rewards and punishments, God rules the world of men. The amount of protection and happy satisfaction assigned to an individual depends on his fulfillment of the ethical demands; his love of God and his consciousness of being loved by God are the foundations of the security with which he is armed against the dangers of the external world and of his human environment. Finally, in prayer he has assured himself a direct influence on the divine will and with it a share in the divine omnipotence...

This being the prehistory of the religious *Weltanschauung*, let us turn now to what has happened since then and to what is still going on before our eyes. The scientific spirit, strengthened by the observation of natural processes, has begun, in the course of time, to treat religion as a human affair and to submit it to a critical examination. Religion was not able to stand up to this. What first gave rise to suspicion and skepticism were its tales of miracles, for they contradicted everything that had been taught by sober observation and betrayed too clearly the influence of the activity of the human imagination. After this its doctrines explaining the origin of the universe met with rejection, for they gave evidence of an ignorance which bore the stamp of ancient times and to which, thanks to their increased familiarity with the laws of nature, people knew they were superior. The idea that the universe came into existence through acts of copulation or creation analogous to the origin of individual people has ceased to be the most obvious and self-evident hypothesis since the distinction between animate creatures with a mind and an inanimate Nature had impressed itself on human thought—a distinction which made it impossible to retain belief in the original animism. Nor must we overlook the influence of the comparative study of different religious systems and the impression of their mutual exclusiveness and intolerance.

Strengthened by these preliminary exercises, the scientific spirit gained enough courage at last to venture on an examination of the most important and emotionally valuable elements of the religious *Weltanschauung*. People may always have seen, though it was long before they dared to say so openly, that the pronouncements of religion promising men protection and happiness if they would only fulfill certain ethical requirements had also shown themselves unworthy of belief. It seems not to be the case that there is a Power in the universe which watches over the well-being of individuals with parental care and brings all their affairs to a happy ending. On the contrary, the destinies of mankind can be brought into harmony neither with the hypothesis of the Universal Benevolence nor with the partly contradictory one of a Universal Justice. Earthquakes, tidal waves, conflagrations, make no distinction between the virtuous and pious and the scoundrel or unbeliever. Even where what is in question is not inanimate Nature but where an individual's fate depends on his relations to other people, it is by no means the rule that virtue is rewarded and that evil finds its punishment. Often enough the violent, cunning or ruthless man seizes the envied good things of the world and the pious man goes away empty. Obscure, unfeeling and unloving powers determine men's fate; the system of rewards and punishments which religion ascribes to the government of the universe seems not to exist. Here once again is a reason for dropping a portion of the animistic theory which has been rescued from animism by religion.

The last contribution to the criticism of the religious *Weltanschauung* was effected by psycho-analysis, by showing how religion originated from the helplessness of children and by tracing its contents to the survival into maturity of the wishes and needs of childhood. This did not precisely mean a contradiction of religion, but it was nevertheless a necessary rounding-off of our knowledge about it, and in one respect at least it was a contradiction, for religion itself lays claim to a divine origin. And to be sure, it is not wrong in this, provided that our interpretation of God is accepted.

In summary, therefore, the judgement of science on the religious *Weltanschauung* is this. While the different religions wrangle with one another as to which of them is in possession of the truth, our view is that the question of the truth of religious beliefs may be left altogether on one side. Religion is an attempt to master the sensory world in which we are situated by means of the wishful world which we have developed within us as a result of biological and psychological necessities. But religion cannot achieve this. Its doctrines bear the imprint of the times in which they arose, the ignorant times of the childhood of humanity. Its consolations deserve no trust. Experience teaches us that the world is no nursery. The ethical demands on which religion seeks to lay stress need, rather, to be given another basis; for they are indispensable to human society and it is dangerous to link obedience to them with religious faith. If we attempt to assign the place of religion in the evolution of mankind, it appears not as a permanent acquisition but as a counterpart to the neurosis which individual civilized men have to go through in their passage from childhood to maturity.[3]

Study and Critical-Thinking Questions

1. According to Freud, there is a "religious world-view" that says religion meets three human psychological needs. What are these three needs?
2. Does Freud believe that God exists and that religion actually does these things? Either way, what is Freud's attitude toward God and religion?

---

3. [The possibility of society suffering from neuroses analogous to individual ones was mentioned by Freud in Chapter VIII of *The Future of an Illusion* (1927c), and near the end of *Civilization and its Discontents* (1930a). He discussed it at much greater length in Essay III, Part I, Section C of *Moses and Monotheism* (1939a). The analogy between religious practices and obsessive actions had been pointed out much earlier (Freud, 1907b).]

3. From where, according to Freud, do human beings get the idea of a father God?
4. From where, according to Freud, do human beings get their moral conscience?
5. Identify at least two religious teachings which Freud believes science has disproved. And how has science disproved them, in Freud's opinion?
6. Cite (*write out*) and explain in your own words the definition of religion ("Religion is…") that Freud gives in the concluding paragraph of this excerpt.
7. What will happen to religion as humanity "matures"? Why?

Questions for Class Discussion

1. What kind of definition (theory) of religion is Freud offering? Is it evaluative (religious or philosophical)? Is it descriptive (phenomenological, historical, functional, or comparative)? Why do you think so? (To be able to respond to this question, you may want to refer back to the piece written by William Young on the study of religion.)
2. What merits would you give to Freud's theory of religion?
3. What are some shortcomings with this theory?
4. How might you illustrate or diagram Freud's theory of religion?

Religion as Ultimate Commitment

Paul Tillich (1886–1965) observed that while some people worship the God of the Bible, others "religiously" devote themselves to making money. He was born in Starzeddel in Germany (today Starosiedle, Poland); his father was a Lutheran pastor. He earned doctorates in philosophy and theology from the Universities of Breslau and Halle, respectively. In 1912, he was ordained a Lutheran minister, and during World War I he served as a military chaplain. After the war, he taught at a number of universities, including the University of Frankfurt. In 1933, he published *The Socialist Decision,* which criticized the dictatorial tendencies of the National Socialist (Nazi) party. Soon thereafter, he emigrated to the United States. From 1934 until his retirement in 1955, he served as professor at Union Theological Seminary in New York. After that, he went on to teach at Harvard University and the University of Chicago.

Tillich set forth his theory of religion in *The Dynamics of Faith* (1957). His thinking about the nature and function of religion may have been influenced by his experience with the Nazi ideology in Germany. Just like the Nazis promised the German people that they would become a great nation, and in turn demanded sacrifice and commitment to the cause of nationhood, so Tillich understood religion and, in particular, the Christian faith, as promising total fulfillment to people, while demanding total commitment from them.

Excerpts from Paul Tillich

The Dynamics of Faith

© Gigraa_Dreamstime.com

FAITH AS ULTIMATE CONCERN

Faith is the state of being ultimately concerned: the dynamics of faith are the dynamics of man's ultimate concern. Man, like every living being, is concerned about many things, above all about those which condition his very existence, such as food and shelter. But man, in contrast to other living beings, has spiritual concerns—cognitive, aesthetic, social, political. Some of them are urgent, often extremely urgent, and each of them as well as the vital concerns can claim ultimacy for a human life or the life of a social group. If it claims ultimacy it demands the total surrender of him who accepts this claim, and it promises total fulfillment even if all other claims have to be subjected to it or rejected in

Excerpts from pp. 1–4, 11–14, 18–21 [2043 words] from DYNAMICS OF FAITH by PAUL TILLICH. Copyright © 1957 by Paul Tillich. Renewed © 1985 by Hannah Tillich. Reprinted by permission of HarperCollins Publishers.

its name. If a national group makes the life and growth of the nation its ultimate concern, it demands that all other concerns, economic wellbeing, health and life, family, aesthetic and cognitive truth, justice and humanity, be sacrificed. The extreme nationalisms of our century are laboratories for the study of what ultimate concern means in all aspects of human existence, including the smallest concern of one's daily life. Everything is centered in the only god, the nation—a god who certainly proves to be a demon, but who shows clearly the unconditional character of an ultimate concern.

But it is not only the unconditional demand made by that which is one's ultimate concern, it is also the promise of ultimate fulfillment which is accepted in the act of faith. The content of this promise is not necessarily defined. It can be expressed in indefinite symbols or in concrete symbols which cannot be taken literally, like the "greatness" of one's nation in which one participates even if one has died for it, or the conquest of mankind by the "saving race," etc. In each of these cases it is "ultimate fulfillment" that is promised, and it is exclusion from such fulfillment which is threatened if the unconditional demand is not obeyed.

An example—and more than an example—is the faith manifest in the religion of the Old Testament. It also has the character of ultimate concern in demand, threat and promise. The content of this concern is not the nation—although Jewish nationalism has sometimes tried to distort it into that—but the content is the God of justice, who, because he represents justice for everybody and every nation, is called the universal God, the God of the universe. He is the ultimate concern of every pious

Jew, and therefore in his name the great commandment is given: "You shall love the Lord your God with all your heart, and with all your soul, and with all your might" (Deut 6:5). This is what ultimate concern means and from these words the term "ultimate concern" is derived. They state unambiguously the character of genuine faith, the demand of total surrender to the subject of ultimate concern. The Old Testament is full of commands which make the nature of this surrender concrete, and it is full of promises and threats in relation to it. Here also are the promises of symbolic indefiniteness, although they center around fulfillment of the national and individual life, and the threat is the exclusion from such fulfillment through national extinction and individual catastrophe. Faith, for the men of the Old Testament, is the state of being ultimately and unconditionally concerned about Jahweh and about what he represents in demand, threat and promise.

Another example—almost a counter-example, yet nevertheless equally revealing—is the ultimate concern with "success" and with social standing and economic power. It is the god of many people in the highly competitive Western culture and it does what every ultimate concern must do: it demands unconditional surrender to its laws even if the price is the sacrifice of genuine human relations, personal conviction, and creative *eros*. Its threat is social and economic defeat, and its promise—indefinite as all such promises—the fulfillment of one's being…

The term "ultimate concern" unites the subjective and the objective side of the act of faith—the *fides qua creditor* (the Faith through which one believes) and the *fides quae creditor* (the faith which is believed). The first is the classical term for the centered act of the personality, the ultimate concern. The second is the classical term for that toward which this act is directed, the ultimate itself, expressed in symbols of the divine. This distinction is very important, but not ultimately so, for the one side cannot be without the other. There is no faith without a content toward which it is directed. There is always something meant in the act of faith. And there is no way of having the content of faith except in the act of faith. All speaking about divine matters which is not done in the state of ultimate concern is meaningless. Because that which is meant in the act of faith cannot be approached in any other way than through an act of faith.

In terms like ultimate, unconditional, infinite, absolute, the difference between subjectivity and objectivity is overcome. The ultimate of the act of faith and the ultimate that is meant in the act of faith are one and the same. This is symbolically expressed by the mystics when they say that their knowledge of God is the knowledge God has of himself; and it is expressed by Paul when he says (I Cor 13) that he will know as he is known, namely, by God. God never can be object without being at the same time subject. Even a successful prayer is, according to Paul (Rom 8), not possible without God as Spirit praying within us. The same experience expressed in abstract language is the disappearance of the ordinary subject-object scheme in the experience of the ultimate, the unconditional. In the act of faith that which is the source of this act is present beyond the cleavage of subject and object. It is present as both and beyond both.

This character of faith gives an additional criterion for distinguishing true and false ultimacy. The finite which claims infinity without having it (as, e.g., a nation or success) is not able to transcend the subject-object scheme. It remains an object which the believer looks at as a subject. He can approach it with ordinary knowledge and subject it to ordinary handling. There are, of course, many degrees in the endless realm of false ultimacies. The nation is nearer to true ultimacy than is success. Nationalistic ecstasy can produce a state in which the subject is almost swallowed by the object. But after a period the subject emerges again, disappointed radically and totally, and by looking at the nation in a skeptical and calculating way does injustice even to its justified claims. The more idolatrous a faith the less it is able to overcome the cleavage between true and idolatrous faith. In true faith the ultimate concern is a concern about the truly ultimate; while in idolatrous faith preliminary, finite realities are elevated to the rank of ultimacy. The inescapable consequence of idolatrous faith is "existential disappointment," a disappointment which penetrates into the very existence of man! This is the dynamics of idolatrous faith: that it is faith, and as such, the centered act of a personality; that the centering point is something which is more or less on to the periphery; and that, therefore, the act of faith leads to a loss of the center and to a disruption of the personality. The ecstatic character of even an idolatrous faith can hide this consequence only for a certain time. But finally it breaks into the open.

FAITH AND DOUBT

We now return to a fuller description of faith as an act of the human personality, as its centered and total act. An act of faith is an act of a finite being who is grasped by and turned to the infinite. It is a finite act with all the limitations of a finite act, and it is an act in which the infinite participates beyond the limitations of a finite act. Faith is certain in so far as it is an experience of the holy. But faith is uncertain in so far as the infinite to which it is related is received by a finite being. This element of uncertainty in faith cannot be removed, it must be accepted. And the element in faith which accepts this is courage. Faith includes an element of immediate awareness which gives certainty and an element of uncertainty. To accept this is courage. In the courageous standing of uncertainty, faith shows most visibly its dynamic character.

If we try to describe the relation of faith and courage, we must use a larger concept of courage than that which is ordinarily used.[4] Courage as an element of faith is the daring self-affirmation of one's own being in spite of the powers of "nonbeing" which are the heritage of everything finite. Where there is daring and courage there is the possibility of failure. And in every act of faith this possibility is present. The risk must be taken. Whoever makes his nation his ultimate concern needs courage in order to maintain this concern. Only certain is the ultimacy as ultimacy, the infinite passion as infinite passion. This is a reality given to the self with his own nature. It is as immediate and as much beyond doubt as the self is to the self. It *is* the self

---

4. Cf. Paul Tillich, *The Courage to Be*. Yale University Press.

in its self-transcending quality. But there is not certainty of this kind about the content of our ultimate concern, be it nation, success, a god, or the God of the Bible: They all are contents without immediate awareness. Their acceptance as matters of ultimate concern is a risk and therefore an act of courage. There is a risk if what was considered as a matter of ultimate concern proves to be a matter of preliminary and transitory concern—as, for example, the nation. The risk to faith in one's ultimate concern is indeed the greatest risk man can run. For if it proves to be a failure, the meaning of one's life breaks down; one surrenders oneself, including truth and justice, to something which is not worth it. One has given away one's personal center without having a chance to regain it. The reaction of despair in people which have experienced the breakdown of their national claims is an irrefutable proof of the idolatrous character of their national concern. In the long run this is the inescapable result of an ultimate concern, the subject matter of which is not ultimate. And this is the risk faith must take; this is the risk which is unavoidable if a finite being affirms itself. Ultimate concern is ultimate risk and ultimate courage. It is not risk and needs no courage with respect to ultimacy itself. But it is risk and demands courage if it affirms a concrete concern. And every faith has a concrete element in itself. It is concerned about something or somebody. But this something or this somebody may prove to be not ultimate at all. Then faith is a failure in its concrete expression, although it is not a failure in the experience of the unconditional itself. A god disappears; divinity remains. Faith risks the vanishing of the concrete god in whom it believes. It may well be that with the vanishing of the god the believer breaks down without being able to re-establish his centered self by a new content of his ultimate concern. This risk cannot be taken away from any act of faith. There is only one point which is a matter not of risk but of immediate certainty and herein lies the greatness and the pain of being human; namely, one's standing between one's finitude and one's potential infinity.

All this is sharply expressed in the relation of faith and doubt. If faith is understood as belief that something is true, doubt is incompatible with the act of faith. If faith is understood as being ultimately concerned, doubt is a necessary element in it. It is a consequence of the risk of faith.

Study and Critical-Thinking Questions

1. How does Tillich define religion? What do you think he means by this phrase? One could say that William Young's definition (first reading in this unit) of religion is rooted in Tillich's theory of religion. What are the parallels?
2. What kinds of things can be ultimate concern/religion? Cite two of the three examples that Tillich gives and explain them in your own words. What are a few other examples of things that can be religion, based on Tillich's theory?
3. In what ways are promises and demands key elements of religion, as defined by Tillich?
4. Explain what two of the ultimate concerns ("religions") you mentioned in your answer to question 2

promises to a person. Explain what each one demands of a person.
5. Explain the connection between demands and promises with an "idolatrous faith" (as discussed by Tillich). And what is the connection between demands and promises with a "true faith" (authentic ultimate concern)?
6. What does Tillich mean by "existential disappointment"? How does existential disappointment relate to idolatrous faith?
7. Some would say that if one has faith, one doesn't have doubt. Tillich says that faith in an ultimate concern (religion) requires doubt (and risk and courage). Why is that the case?

Questions for Class Discussion

1. What kind of definition (theory) of religion is Tillich offering? Is it evaluative (religious or philosophical)? Is it descriptive (phenomenological, historical, functional, or comparative)? Why do you think so? (To be able to respond to this question, you may want to refer back to the previous piece written by William Young on the study of religion.)
2. What merits would you give to Tillich's theory of religion?
3. What are some shortcomings of this theory?
4. How might you illustrate or diagram Tillich's theory of religion?

UNIT TWO:
Five Religious Traditions

...honor another's religion, for doing so strengthens both one's own and that of the other.
— *Emperor Ashoka, Third Century BCE*

If I went back to college today, I think I would probably major in comparative religion, because that's how integrated it is in everything that we are working on and deciding and thinking about today.
— *United States Secretary of State John Kerry, August 7, 2013*

As the two quotes above demonstrate, a recognition of diverse religious perspectives, as well as the necessity to understand these diverse religious perspectives, extends over millennia—at least five thousand years in the scope of the two quotes above. In addition, as the two aforementioned quotes also demonstrate, this understanding is essential on both a personal level and a global level.

In this unit, "Five Religious Traditions," you will be directed to a resource that not only offers some basic information for the five traditions introduced in this chapter, but also goes beyond those five traditions and even beyond your use of this book. You will be familiarizing yourself with a resource to which you may come back in the future in your navigation of the waters of religious diversity. The Pluralism Project is a project of Harvard University and is a two-decade-long research project to engage students in studying the new religious diversity in the United States. You are encouraged to explore the site (http://pluralism.org) beyond the suggested readings in this brief introductory chapter.

Hinduism

© Georgios Kollidas_Dreamstime.com

If I were asked to define the Hindu creed, I should simply say:
Search after truth through non-violent means.
A man may not believe in God and still call himself a Hindu.
Hinduism is a relentless pursuit after truth...
Hinduism is the religion of truth. Truth is God.
Denial of God we have known.
Denial of truth we have not known.

— *Mahatma Gandhi*

"Religion is when a group of people who believe the same thing get together and study the same holy book and worship the same God." When I, as a teacher, invite students to write out their definition of religion at the beginning of an Introduction to Religion course, I often read statements similar to this. It is certainly a concise and comprehensive definition. However, as I begin teaching Hinduism, I choose to begin with a discussion of what Hinduism is *not*. Hinduism is *not* a common belief, nor a common book, nor a common God, nor a common worship, nor even necessarily a common congregation or gathering. This blows the sides out of the neatly wrapped box of "what religion is." As you read the recommended material, let the sides of your "this is religion" box be pliable. Otherwise, you will be trying to squeeze something (Hinduism) into a box into which it cannot fit (many of our notions of "religion").

SUGGESTED READINGS

Go to: **pluralism.org**

- **Religion** link at top right under On Common Ground
- **RELIGION** on left menu bar
- **HINDUISM** box

- **Introduction to Hinduism** (left menu bar): read the following links/pages:
  — The Textures of Tradition
  — What does "Hindu" mean?
  — A Context for Diversity
  — Many Gods and One
  — Veda: Scripture and Authority
  — Brahman and Atman: That Art Thou
  — Bhakti: The Way of Devotion
  — Karma: The Way of Action
  — Dharma: The Social Order

- **The Hindu Experience** (left menu bar): read the following links/pages:
  — Home Altar
  — Ganesha: Lord of the Beginnings

TERMS FOR STUDY

1. Aryan people
2. Atman
3. Bhagavad-Gita
4. Bhakti
5. Brahman
6. Brahmin
7. Castes
8. Dharma
9. Ganesha
10. Hindu
11. Jnana
12. Karma
13. Sanskrit
14. Upanishads
15. Vedas

Buddhism

© Zoom-zoom_Dreamstime.com

A man is not called wise because he talks and talks again; but if he is peaceful, loving and fearless then he is in truth called wise.

—*Gautama Buddha,*
The Dhammapada: The Sayings of the Buddha

Letting go gives us freedom, and freedom is the only condition for happiness. If, in our heart, we still cling to anything—anger, anxiety, or possessions—we cannot be free.
—Thích Nhất Hanh, *The Heart of the Buddha's Teaching: Transforming Suffering into Peace, Joy, and Liberation*

Religion always points toward a God or Higher Being, right? Your introduction to Buddhism will show you that this is not always the case. Buddhism, in its pure form, does not espouse any God or Higher Power. Certainly, one may find Buddhists who make offerings and prayers to gods, but these are typically blending folk religion with Buddhist teaching. One Buddhist teacher explained that while Buddhists may pray to and make offerings to gods for material needs, gods are of no aid on the path to enlightenment and salvation. As a matter of fact, the Buddha (Siddartha) was raised in the Hindu tradition, but left that tradition seeking a way to escape the perpetual rebirth into a life of suffering, a rebirth that is largely determined by one's devotion to gods and goddesses. Therefore, Buddhism is often best-described as a philosophy of life, rather than a spiritual path.

SUGGESTED READINGS

Go to: **pluralism.org**

- **Religion** link at top right under On Common Ground
- **RELIGION** on left menu bar
- **BUDDHISM** box
- **Introduction to Buddhism** (left menu bar): read all ten links/pages in this section
- **The Buddhist Experience** (left menu bar): read the following three links/pages
  — The Image of the Buddha
  — The Practice of Mindfulness
  — Buddha's Birthday

TERMS FOR STUDY

1. Arahant
2. Bodhi
3. Bodhisattva
4. Buddha
5. the Dharma
6. Duhka
7. Eight-Fold Path
8. Four Noble Truths
9. Mahayana
10. Mara
11. Nirvana
12. Pali canon
13. Queen Maya
14. Sangha
15. Siddartha
16. Theravada
17. Three Treasures
18. Vajrayana

Judaism

© Alexey Karpenko_Dreamstime.com

The pursuit of knowledge for its own sake, an almost fanatical love of justice and the desire for personal independence—these are the features of the Jewish tradition which make me thank my stars that I belong to it.
—*Albert Einstein, The World As I See It*

That which is hateful to you, do not do to your fellow. That is the whole Torah; the rest is the explanation; go and learn.
— *Hillel the Elder, Jewish scholar and sage, lived 110 BCE–7 CE*

Judaism is the oldest of the major monotheistic traditions, which include Christianity and Islam. In my classes, I often draw (poorly) a trunk of a tree with three branches extending from it. The trunk represents ancient Judaism. One branch represents modern Judaism, another Christianity, and the third branch represents Islam. All three of these diverse expressions of religion are built upon the foundation of the prophets and the ethical monotheism of ancient Israelite religion as expressed in the Hebrew Bible (the Old Testament). Yet, modern Judaism is not the religious practice of the ancient Israelites. Ancient Israelite religion was centered on the successive Jerusalem Temples, the last of which was destroyed in the first century C.E. Therefore, the stories and ethical teaching of the Hebrew Bible endure, but much of the ritual practice of Judaism has over the years yielded to the teaching of the rabbis. Thus, if you have read the Old Testament and therefore think that you understand Judaism, that is not the case; therefore, you are encouraged to read on.

SUGGESTED READINGS

Go to: **pluralism.org**

- **Religion** link at top right under On Common Ground
- **RELIGION** on left menu bar
- **JUDAISM** box
- **Introduction to Judaism** (left menu bar): read all, EXCEPT the following links/pages:
  — Israel: Jewish Nationhood
  — Diaspora Community
  — Modern Jewish Culture
- **The Jewish Experience** (left menu bar): read the following links/pages:
  — Keeping Shabbat
  — Rosh Hashanah and Yom Kippur
  — Hanukkah
  — Passover
  — Bar and Bat Mitzvah

TERMS FOR STUDY

1. Abraham
2. Bar Mitzvah
3. Bat Mitzvah
4. Gemarah
5. Hanukkah
6. Holocaust
7. Kabbalah
8. Kosher/Kashrut
9. Mishnah
10. Passover/Pesach
11. Rosh Hashanah
12. Shabbat
13. Talmud
14. Torah
15. Yom Kippur
16. Zionism

Christianity

© Taiga_Dreamstime.com

Reality, in fact, is usually something you could not have guessed. That is one of the reasons I believe Christianity. It is a religion you could not have guessed. If it offered us just the kind of universe we had always expected, I should feel we were making it up. But, in fact, it is not the sort of thing anyone would have made up. It has just that queer twist about it that real things have.

— C.S. Lewis, *Mere Christianity*

Truth, according to the Christian faith, is the love of God for us in Jesus Christ. Therefore, truth is a relationship.

— *Pope Francis, "Letter to a Non-Believer: Pope Francis Responds to Dr. Eugenio Scalfari, Journalist of 'La Repubblica'"*

Christianity is quite diverse and may be found all over the world. Yet, its foundation is the life, teaching, death, and reported resurrection of Jesus, a Jew who lived in the first century C.E. Jesus lived and moved and taught within the Jewish tradition his whole life, right up until the end when he made a fateful journey to Jerusalem to observe the Jewish Passover, a journey that ended in his execution by crucifixion. Although Jesus did not write any sort of religious treatise, as far as we know, stories of his life and his teachings were eventually recorded as *Gospels*, four of which may be found in the New Testament. If there is a creedal statement offered in the Gospels, it is simply that "Jesus is the Messiah, the son of the living God" (Matthew 16:16). Over the years, this simple confession of faith has given rise to great variation in doctrine and practice as Christianity has spread from Jerusalem in the first century to around the globe in the twenty-first.

SUGGESTED READINGS

Go to: **pluralism.org**

- **Religion** link at top right under On Common Ground
- **RELIGION** on left menu bar
- **CHRISTIANITY** box
- **Introduction to Christianity** (left menu bar): read the following links/pages:
  — Orthodox Christian Churches
  — The Roman Catholic Church
  — The Protestant Movement
- **The Christian Experience** (left menu bar): read the following links/pages:
  — Sharing the Bread of Life
  — Advent and Christmas
  — Ash Wednesday and Easter Sunday
  — Baptism by Water and Spirit

TERMS FOR STUDY

1. Advent
2. Baptism
3. Christmas
4. Easter
5. Eucharist, or Communion
6. Icons
7. Lent
8. Martin Luther
9. Orthodox Christian Churches
10. Protestant Movement
11. Roman Catholic Church
12. Theosis

Islam

© Joanne Zh_Dreamstime.com

O mankind! We created you from a single soul, male and female, and made you into nations and tribes, so that you may come to know one another. Truly, the most honored of you in God's sight is the greatest of you in piety. God is All-Knowing, All Aware.

— *Qur'an 49:13*

None of you [truly] believes until he wishes for his brother what he wishes for himself.

—*The Prophet Muhammed, as narrated and recorded in Hadith 13*

Islam is the most recently developed of the major religious traditions, rooted in the teachings of the Prophet Muhammed (c. 570–632 C.E.). Yet, Islam's roots may be traced to ancient times, to Abraham (*Ibrahim*) and his son Ishmael (*Ismail*). Islam is rooted in two fundamental beliefs that are stated in the creed, or *shahada*, of Islam:

"There is no God but God, and Muhammed is the Messenger of God." Thus, all Muslims declare a strict monotheism alongside the centrality of Muhammed as God's final messenger to the world. The message from God (*Allah*) is recorded in the Qur'an, the sacred text of Islam. The Hadith, quoted above, is a collection of the sayings and actions of Muhammed as narrated by family and followers. Though not considered a sacred text, the Hadith, along with the Qur'an, provide guidance in all areas of life for Muslims today.

SUGGESTED READINGS

Go to: **pluralism.org**

- **Religion** link at top right under On Common Ground
- **RELIGION** on left menu bar
- **ISLAM** box
- **Introduction to Islam** (left menu bar): read the following links/pages:
  — The Call of Islam
  — Islam Means Being "Muslim"
  — Qur'an: the Word of God
  — Muhammad: the Messenger of God
  — Sunni and Shi'a Interpretations
  — Sufism: Seeking God
  — Shari'ah: Following the Straight Path
  — The Five Pillars
- **The Muslim Experience** (left menu bar): read the following links/pages:
  — The Call to Prayer
  — Becoming a Muslim
  — Halal Food

TERMS FOR STUDY

1. Ali
2. Allah
3. Five pillars
4. Hajj
5. Halal
6. Haram
7. Hijrah
8. Islam
9. Ka'bah
10. Madinah (Medina)
11. Makkah (Mecca)
12. Muhammad
13. Muslim
14. Qur'an
15. Ramadan (sawm)
16. Shari'ah law
17. Shi'ah Muslims
18. Sufism
19. Sunni Muslims

UNIT THREE:
Ethical Decision-Making

All major religions have love and compassion at their core, they promote tolerance not violence and hate, and most have their own version of the Golden Rule—treat others as you wish to be treated. They all recognize that human happiness ultimately comes from our relationship with one another.

— *Desmond Tutu, South African social rights activist, retired Anglican bishop, 1984 Nobel Peace Prize, 2009 Presidential Medal of Freedom*

We know that whatever our differences, there is one law that binds all great religions together. Jesus told us to "love thy neighbor as thyself." The Torah commands, "That which is hateful to you, do not do to your fellow." In Islam, there is a hadith that reads "None of you truly believes until he wishes for his brother what he wishes for himself." And the same is true for Buddhists and Hindus; for followers of Confucius and for humanists. It is, of course, the Golden Rule—the call to love one another; to treat with dignity and respect those with whom we share a brief moment on this earth. It is an ancient rule; a simple rule; but also one of the most challenging. For it asks each of us to take some measure of responsibility for the well-being of people we may not know or worship with or agree with on every issue. Sometimes, it asks us to reconcile with bitter enemies or to resolve ancient hatreds. It requires us not only to believe, but to do—to give something of ourselves for the benefit of others and the betterment of the world. In this way, the particular faith that motivates each of us can promote a greater good for all of us."

— *President Barack Obama, National Prayer Breakfast, February 5, 2009*

Can one have a code of ethics without having religion? Certainly, this question is continually under debate. One of the readings in this unit, written by Tibetan Buddhism's Dalai Lama, addresses this very question. His answer may be surprising to you. In addition, Paul Tillich's theory of religion (Unit One reading) asserts that all people are religious, because all have some object, person, belief, or goal that holds a place of ultimacy in their lives—something about which they are "religious." To extrapolate from Tillich's theory then, their ethical decisions are rooted in their "religion," that is to say, that object, person, belief, or goal which is their primary arbiter of decision-making.

Then, there is the flip side of this question: Can religion exist without an ethical code? One would be hard-pressed to find a religion that does not contain an ethical component. All do. And, surprisingly to many, there are even some ethical instructions that are shared among all religious traditions. Most notably, and as at least two of the suggested readings in this unit assert, the ethical principle that is often called The Golden Rule is expressed in some way in every major religious tradition: *Do unto others as you would have them do unto you.*

This unit is intended to briefly introduce you to ideas about ethics from various viewpoints: Judeo-Christian (Joseph Fletcher), Islamic (Qur'an texts), and Buddhist.

Love is the Supreme Law

Treat not others in ways that you yourself would find hurtful.
— *Udana-Varga 5.18 (Hinduism)*

Teach this triple truth to all: ... a life of service and compassion are the things which renew humanity.
— *Siddartha (Buddhism)*

... love your neighbor as yourself.
— *Leviticus 19:18 (Judaism)*

What is hateful to you, do not to your fellow man."
— *Talmud (Islam)*

Jesus replied, ... 'Love your neighbor as yourself.'
— *Matthew 22:39 (Christianity)*

In Joseph Fletcher's book *Situation Ethics*, he lays out a clear approach to both simple and complex ethical problems. Though written as a perspective on Christian ethics, this approach has become applicable within all major religious traditions. His ethical philosophy? *Love is the only norm.* Should that sound too simplistic or slippery, other chapters in the book discuss what love is (i.e., justice)—and is not (i.e., liking someone). In this excerpt from the first chapter of the book, he discusses the pitfalls of approaching life's decisions with no guiding principles (antinomianism) or with purely legalistic principles. His assertion is that "acting responsibly with love" is the best approach.

Excerpts from Joseph Fletcher

Situation Ethics: The New Morality

© Paulpaladin_Dreamstime.com

There are at bottom only three alternative routes or approaches to follow in making moral decisions. They are: (1) the legalistic; (2) the antinomian, the opposite extreme—i.e., a lawless or unprincipled approach; and (3) the situational. All three have played their part in the history of Western morals, legalism being by far the most common and persistent. Just as legalism triumphed among the Jews after the exile, so, in spite of Jesus' and Paul's revolt against it, it has managed to dominate Christianity constantly from very early days. . . .

From *Situation Ethics: The New Morality* by Joseph Fletcher. Copyright © 1966 by Westminster John Knox Press. Reprinted by permission. (pp. 17–18, 22–23, 26, 31, 33)

Three Approaches to Decision-Making

1. Legalism

With this approach one enters into every decision-making situation encumbered with a whole apparatus of prefabricated rules and regulations. Not just the spirit but the letter of the law reigns. Its principles, codified in rules, are not merely guidelines or maxims to illuminate the situation; they are *directives* to be followed. Solutions are preset, and you can "look them up" in a book—a Bible or a confessor's manual.

Judaism, Catholicism, Protestantism—all major Western religious traditions have been legalistic. In morals as in doctrine they have kept to a spelled-out, "systematic" orthodoxy. The ancient Jews, especially under the post-exilic Maccabean and Pharisaic leadership, lived by the law or Torah, and its oral tradition (halakah).[1] It was a code of 613 (or 621) precepts, amplified by an increasingly complicated mass of Mishnaic interpretations and applications.

Statutory and code law inevitably piles up, ruling upon ruling, because the complications of life and the claims of mercy and compassion combine—even with code legalists—to accumulate an elaborate system of exceptions and compromise, in the form of rules for breaking the rules! ...

---

1. The prophetic J tradition gave way to the E-D tradition, with its precepts and laws.

2. Antinomianism

Over against legalism, as a sort of polar opposite, we can put antinomianism. This is the approach with which one enters into the decision-making situation armed with no principles or maxims whatsoever, to say nothing of *rules*. In every "existential moment" or "unique" situation, it declares, one must rely upon the situation of itself, *there and then,* to provide its ethical solution. . . .

While legalists are preoccupied with law and its stipulations, the Gnostics [a type of antinomianism] are so flatly opposed to law—even in principle—that their moral decisions are random, unpredictable, erratic, quite anomalous. Making moral decisions is a matter of spontaneity; it is literally unprincipled, purely *ad hoc* and casual. They follow no forecastable course from one situation to another. They are, exactly, anarchic—i.e., without a rule. They are not only "unbound by the chains of law" but actually sheer extemporizers, impromptu and intellectually irresponsible. They not only cast the old Torah [Jewish Law] aside; they even cease to think seriously and *carefully* about the demands of love as it has been shown in Christ, the love norm itself. . . .

3. Situationism

A third approach, in between legalism and antinomian unprincipledness, is situation ethics. (To jump from one polarity to the other would be only to go from the frying pan to the fire.) The situationist enters into every decision-making situation fully armed with the ethical maxims of his community and its heritage, and he treats them with respect as illuminators of his problems. Just the same he is prepared in any situation to compromise them or set them aside *in the situation* if love seems better served by doing so.

Situation ethics goes part of the way with natural law, by accepting reason as the instrument of moral judgment, while rejecting the notion that the good is "given" in the nature of things, objectively. It goes part of the way with Scriptural law by accepting revelation as the source of the norm while rejecting all "revealed" norms or laws but the one command—to love God in the neighbor. The situationist follows a moral law or violates it according to love's need.

In non-Christian situation ethics some other highest good or *summum bonum* will, of course, take love's place as the one and only standard—such as self-realization in the ethics of Aristotle. But the *Christian* is neighbor-centered first and last. Love is for people, not for principles; i.e., it is personal—and therefore when the impersonal universal conflicts with the personal particular, the latter prevails in situation ethics. Because of its mediating position, prepared to act on moral laws or in spite of them, the antinomians will call situationists soft legalists, and legalists will call them cryptoantinomians.

Principles, Yes, but Not Rules. It is necessary to insist that situation ethics is willing to make full and respectful use of principles, to be treated as maxims but not as laws or precepts. We might call it "principled relativism." To repeat the term used above, principles or maxims or general rules are *illuminators*. But they are not *directors*. The classic rule of moral theology has been to follow laws but do it *as much as possible* according to love and according to reason. Situation ethics, on the other hand, calls upon us to keep law in a subservient place, so that *only* love and reason really count when the chips are down! ...

Nevertheless, in situation ethics even the most revered principles may be thrown aside if they conflict in any concrete case with love. Even Karl Barth, who writes vehemently of "absolutely wrong" actions, allows for what he calls the *ultima ratio*, the outside chance that love in a particular situation might override the absolute. The instance he gives is abortion.[2]

Using terms made popular by Tillich and others, we may say that Christian situationism is a method that proceeds, so to speak, from (1) its one and only law, *agape* (love), to (2) the *sophia* (wisdom) of the church and culture, containing many "general rules" of more or less reliability, to (3) the *kairos* (moment of decision, the fullness of time) in which *the responsible self in the situation* decides whether the *sophia* can serve love there, or not. This is the situational strategy in capsule form. To legalists it will seem to treat the *sophia* without enough reverence and obedience; to antinomians it will appear befuddled and "inhibited" by the *sophia*.

Legalists make an idol of the *sophia*, antinomians repudiate it, situationists *use* it. They cannot give to any principles less than love more than tentative consideration, for they know, with Dietrich Bonhoeffer, "The question of the good is posed and is decided in the midst of each definite, yet unconcluded, unique and transient situation of our lives, in the midst of our living relationships with men, things, institutions and powers, in other words

---

2. *Church Dogmatics* (Edinburgh: T. & T. Clark, 1961), Vol. III, Bk. 4, pp. 420–421.

in the midst of our historical existence."[3] And Bonhoeffer, of course, is a modern Christian ethicist who was himself executed for trying to kill, even *murder*, Adolf Hitler—so far did he go as a situationist.

Study and Critical-Thinking Questions

1. What are the three alternative routes to follow in making ethical decisions, according to Fletcher?
2. As you read the section on legalism make note of
   a. what legalism is, and
   b. Fletcher's critiques of legalism.
3. As you read the section on antinomianism, make note of
   a. what antinomianism is, and
   b. Fletcher's critiques of antinomianism.
4. From the section on situationism:
   a. The situationist enters every decision-making situation with what considerations?
   b. For the Christian situationist, what is the one binding and unexceptionable law?
   c. According to Fletcher, "only _____ and _____ count when the chips are down!"
   d. How does Fletcher describe the three steps of a situationist's strategy or method?
   e. What does Fletcher say about the three different ethical approaches and their relationship to wisdom (*sophia*) or reason?

---

3. *Ethics*, tr. by N. H. Smith (The Macmillan Company, 1955), p. 8.

Texts about WOMEN and about JIHAD in the QURAN

English Translation by Abdullah Yusuf Ali (1938)

(This is not an inclusive list of texts on these topics, but should be representative.)

© 2014 Raisman. Used under license from Shutterstock, Inc.

WOMEN

221. Do not marry unbelieving women (idolaters), until they believe: A slave woman who believes is better than an unbelieving woman, even though she allures you. Nor marry (your girls) to unbelievers until they believe: A man slave who believes is better than an unbeliever, even though he allures you. Unbelievers do (but) beckon you to the Fire. But Allah beckons by His Grace to the Garden (of bliss) and forgiveness, and makes His Signs clear to mankind: That they may celebrate His praise.

222. They ask thee concerning women's courses. Say: They are a hurt and a pollution: So keep away from women in their courses, and do not approach them until they are clean. But when they have purified themselves, ye may approach them in any manner, time, or place ordained for you by Allah. For Allah loves those who turn to Him constantly and He loves those who keep themselves pure and clean.

223. Your wives are as a tilth unto you; so approach your tilth when or how ye will; but do some good act for your souls beforehand; and fear Allah. And know that ye are to meet Him (in the Hereafter), and give (these) good tidings to those who believe. (2:221–223)

226. For those who take an oath for abstention from their wives, a waiting for four months is ordained; if then they return, Allah is Oft-forgiving, Most Merciful.

227. But if their intention is firm for divorce, Allah heareth and knoweth all things.

228. Divorced women shall wait concerning themselves for three monthly periods. Nor is it lawful for them to hide what Allah Hath created in their wombs, if they have faith in Allah and the Last Day. And their husbands have the better right to take them back in that period, if they wish for reconciliation. And women shall have rights similar to the rights against them, according to what is equitable; but men have a degree (of advantage) over them. And Allah is Exalted in Power, Wise.

229. A divorce is only permissible twice: after that, the parties should either hold Together on equitable terms, or separate with kindness. It is not lawful for you, (Men), to take back any of your gifts (from your wives), except when both parties fear that they would be unable to keep the limits ordained by Allah. If ye (judges) do indeed fear that they would be unable to keep the limits ordained by Allah, there is no blame on either of them if she give something for her freedom. These are the limits ordained by Allah. So do not transgress them if any do transgress the limits ordained by Allah, such persons wrong (Themselves as well as others).

230. So if a husband divorces his wife (irrevocably), He cannot, after that, re-marry her until after she has married another husband and He has divorced her. In that case there is no blame on either of them if they re-unite, provided they feel that they can keep the limits ordained by Allah. Such are the limits ordained by Allah, which He makes plain to those who understand.

231. When ye divorce women, and they fulfil the term of their ('Iddat), either take them back on equitable terms or set them free on equitable terms; but do not take them back to injure them, (or) to take undue advantage; if any one does that; He wrongs his own soul. Do not treat Allah's signs as a jest, but solemnly rehearse Allah's favours on you, and the fact that He sent down to you the Book and Wisdom, for your instruction. And fear Allah, and know that Allah is well acquainted with all things.

232. When ye divorce women, and they fulfil the term of their ('Iddat), do not prevent them from marrying their (former) husbands, if they mutually agree on equitable terms. This instruction is for all amongst you, who believe in Allah and the Last Day. That is (the course Making for) most virtue and purity amongst you and Allah knows, and ye know not.

233. The mothers shall give such to their offspring for two whole years, if the father desires to complete the term. But he shall bear the cost of their food and clothing on equitable terms. No soul shall have a burden laid on it greater than it can bear. No mother shall be treated unfairly on account of her child. Nor father on account of his child, an heir shall be chargeable in the same way. If they both decide on weaning, by mutual consent, and after due consultation, there is no blame on them. If ye decide on a foster-mother for your offspring, there is no blame on you, provided ye pay (the mother) what ye offered, on equitable terms. But fear Allah and know that Allah sees well what ye do.

234. If any of you die and leave widows behind, they shall wait concerning themselves four months and ten days: When they have fulfilled their term, there is no blame on you if they dispose of themselves in a just and reasonable manner. And Allah is well acquainted with what ye do.

235. There is no blame on you if ye make an offer of betrothal or hold it in your hearts. Allah knows that ye cherish them in your hearts: But do not make a secret contract with them except in terms Honourable, nor resolve on the tie of marriage till the term prescribed is fulfilled. And know that Allah Knoweth what is in your hearts, and take heed of Him; and know that Allah is Oft-forgiving, Most Forbearing.

236. There is no blame on you if ye divorce women before consummation or the fixation of their dower; but bestow on them (A suitable gift), the wealthy according to his means, and the poor according to his means;- A gift of a reasonable amount is due from those who wish to do the right thing.

237. And if ye divorce them before consummation, but after the fixation of a dower for them, then the half of the dower (Is due to them), unless they remit it or (the man's half) is remitted by him in whose hands is the marriage tie; and the remission (of the man's half) is the nearest to righteousness. And do not forget Liberality between yourselves. For Allah sees well all that ye do. (2:226–237)

195. And their Lord hath accepted of them, and answered them: "Never will I suffer to be lost the work of any of you, be he male or female: Ye are members, one of another: Those who have left their homes, or been driven out therefrom, or suffered harm in My Cause, or fought or been slain,- verily, I will blot out from them their iniquities, and admit them into Gardens with rivers flowing beneath;- A reward from the presence of Allah, and from His presence is the best of rewards." (3:195, Yusuf Ali).

4. And give the women (on marriage) their dower as a free gift; but if they, of their own good pleasure, remit any part of it to you, Take it and enjoy it with right good cheer.

7. From what is left by parents and those nearest related there is a share for men and a share for women, whether the property be small or large,-a determinate share. (4:4,7, Yusuf Ali)

19. O ye who believe! Ye are forbidden to inherit women against their will. Nor should ye treat them with harshness, that ye may Take away part of the dower ye have given them,-except where they have been guilty of open lewdness; on the contrary live with them on a footing of kindness and equity. If ye take a dislike to them it may be that ye dislike a thing, and Allah brings about through it a great deal of good.

20. But if ye decide to take one wife in place of another, even if ye had given the latter a whole treasure for dower, Take not the least bit of it back: Would ye take it by slander and manifest wrong?

21. And how could ye take it when ye have gone in unto each other, and they have Taken from you a solemn covenant?

22. And marry not women whom your fathers married,- except what is past: It was shameful and odious,- an abominable custom indeed.

23. Prohibited to you (For marriage) are:- Your mothers, daughters, sisters; father's sisters, Mother's sisters; brother's daughters, sister's daughters; foster-mothers (Who gave you suck), foster-sisters; your wives' mothers; your step-daughters under your guardianship, born of your wives to whom ye have gone in,- no prohibition if ye have not gone in;- (Those who have been) wives of your sons proceeding from your loins; and two sisters in wedlock at one and the same time, except for what is past; for Allah is Oft-forgiving, Most Merciful;-

24. Also (prohibited are) women already married, except those whom your right hands possess: Thus hath Allah ordained (Prohibitions) against you: Except for these, all others are lawful, provided ye seek (them in marriage) with gifts from your property,- desiring chastity, not lust, seeing that ye derive benefit from them, give them their dowers (at least) as prescribed; but if, after a dower is prescribed, agree Mutually (to vary it), there is no blame on you, and Allah is All-knowing, All-wise.

25. If any of you have not the means wherewith to wed free believing women, they may wed believing girls from among those whom your right hands possess: And Allah hath full knowledge about your faith. Ye are one from another: Wed them with the leave of their owners, and give them their dowers, according to what is reasonable: They should be chaste, not lustful, nor taking paramours: when they are taken in wedlock, if they fall into shame, their punishment is half that for free women. This (permission) is for those among you who fear sin; but it is better for you that ye practise self-restraint. And Allah is Oft-forgiving, Most Merciful. (4:19–25, Yusuf Ali)

32. And in no wise covet those things in which Allah Hath bestowed His gifts More freely on some of you than on others: To men is allotted what they earn, and to women what they earn: But ask Allah of His bounty. For Allah hath full knowledge of all things.

33. To (benefit) every one, We have appointed shares and heirs to property left by parents and relatives. To those, also, to whom your right hand was pledged, give their due portion. For truly Allah is witness to all things.

34. Men are the protectors and maintainers of women, because Allah has given the one more (strength) than the other, and because they support them from their means. Therefore the righteous women are devoutly obedient, and guard in (the husband's) absence what Allah would have them guard. As to those women on whose part ye fear disloyalty and ill-conduct, admonish them (first), (Next), refuse to share their beds, (And last) beat them (lightly); but if they return to obedience, seek not against them Means (of annoyance): For Allah is Most High, great (above you all).

35. If ye fear a breach between them twain, appoint (two) arbiters, one from his family, and the other from hers; if they wish for peace, Allah will cause their reconciliation: For Allah hath full knowledge, and is acquainted with all things. (4:32–35, Yusuf Ali)

19. "O Adam! dwell thou and thy wife in the Garden, and enjoy (its good things) as ye wish: but approach not this tree, or ye run into harm and transgression."

20. Then began Satan to whisper suggestions to them, bringing openly before their minds all their shame that was hidden from them (before): he said: "Your Lord only forbade you this tree, lest ye should become angels or such beings as live forever."

21. And he swore to them both, that he was their sincere adviser.

22. So by deceit he brought about their fall: when they tasted of the tree, their shame became manifest to them, and they began to sew together the leaves of the garden over their bodies. And their Lord called unto them: "Did I not forbid you that tree, and tell you that Satan was an avowed enemy unto you?"

23. They said: "Our Lord! We have wronged our own souls: If thou forgive us not and bestow not upon us Thy Mercy, we shall certainly be lost." (7:19:23, Yusuf Ali)

71. The Believers, men and women, are protectors one of another: they enjoin what is just, and forbid what is evil: they observe regular prayers, practise regular charity, and obey Allah and His Messenger. On them will Allah pour His mercy: for Allah is Exalted in power, Wise.

72. Allah hath promised to Believers, men and women, gardens under which rivers flow, to dwell therein, and beautiful mansions in gardens of everlasting bliss. But the greatest bliss is the good pleasure of Allah. That is the supreme felicity. (9:71–72, Yusuf Ali).

30. Say to the believing men that they should lower their gaze and guard their modesty: that will make for greater purity for them: And Allah is well acquainted with all that they do.

31. And say to the believing women that they should lower their gaze and guard their modesty; that they should not display their beauty and ornaments except what (must ordinarily) appear thereof; that they should draw their veils over their bosoms and not display their beauty except to their husbands, their fathers, their husband's fathers, their sons, their husbands' sons, their brothers or their brothers' sons, or their sisters' sons, or their women, or the slaves whom their right hands possess, or male servants free of physical needs, or small children who have no sense of the shame of sex; and that they should not strike their feet in order to draw attention to their hidden ornaments. And O ye Believers! Turn ye all together towards Allah, that ye may attain Bliss. (24:30,31)

13. O mankind! We created you from a single (pair) of a male and a female, and made you into nations and tribes, that ye may know each other (not that ye may despise) (each other). Verily the most honoured of you in the sight of Allah is (he who is) the most righteous of you. And Allah has full knowledge and is well acquainted (with all things). (49:13, Yusuf Ali)

JIHAD

190. Fight in the cause of Allah those who fight you, but do not transgress limits; for Allah loveth not transgressors.

191. And slay them wherever ye catch them, and turn them out from where they have Turned you out; for tumult and oppression are worse than slaughter; but fight them not at the Sacred Mosque, unless they (first) fight you there; but if they fight you, slay them. Such is the reward of those who suppress faith.

192. But if they cease, Allah is Oft-forgiving, Most Merciful.

193. And fight them on until there is no more Tumult or oppression, and there prevail justice and faith in Allah, but if they cease, Let there be no hostility except to those who practice oppression. (2:190–193)

169. Think not of those who are slain in Allah's way as

dead. Nay, they live, finding their sustenance in the presence of their Lord.

170. They rejoice in the bounty provided by Allah. And with regard to those left behind, who have not yet joined them (in their bliss), the (Martyrs) glory in the fact that on them is no fear, nor have they (cause to) grieve.

171. They glory in the Grace and the bounty from Allah, and in the fact that Allah suffereth not the reward of the Faithful to be lost (in the least). (3:169–171)

35. O ye who believe! Do your duty to Allah, seek the means of approach unto Him, and strive with might and main in his cause: that ye may prosper. (5:35)

6. If one amongst the Pagans ask thee for asylum, grant it to him, so that he may hear the word of Allah, and then escort him to where he can be secure. That is because they are men without knowledge. (9:6)

20. Those who believe, and suffer exile and strive with might and main, in Allah's cause, with their goods and their persons, have the highest rank in the sight of Allah, they are the people who will achieve (salvation).

21. Their Lord doth give them glad tidings of a Mercy from Himself, of His good pleasure, and of gardens for them, wherein are delights that endure.

22. They will dwell therein forever. Verily in Allah's presence is a reward, the greatest (of all). (9:20-22)

7. It may be that Allah will grant love (and friendship) between you and those whom ye (now) hold as enemies. For Allah has power (over all things); And Allah is Oft-

Forgiving, Most Merciful.

8. Allah forbids you not, with regard to those who fight you not for (your) Faith nor drive you out of your homes, from dealing kindly and justly with them: for Allah loveth those who are just.

9. Allah only forbids you, with regard to those who fight you for (your) Faith, and drive you out of your homes, and support (others) in driving you out, from turning to them (for friendship and protection). It is such as turn to them (in these circumstances), that do wrong. (60:7–9)

Study and Critical-Thinking Questions

WOMEN texts:
Make a "Top Ten List" of instructions about women from the Quran.
For each of your ten, be sure to note the chapter (*surah*) and verse to which you are referring. For example, (2:226).

JIHAD texts:
What instructions are given as far as:
1. Actions (things to do)
2. Prohibitions (things not to do)
3. Attitudes (motivations) for jihad? Try to list at least 3 for ***each*** of the items listed. Again, indicate the chapter (*surah*) and verse to which you are referring.

Ethics without Religion?

His Holiness the 14th Dalai Lama (b. 1935) is the spiritual leader of Tibet. He received a monastic education and earned the Geshe Lharampa degree, which is equivalent to a doctorate in Buddhist philosophy. After Tibet was invaded by China in 1949/50, the Dalai Lama held peace talks with Chinese leaders. He escaped into exile when a Tibetan uprising against the Chinese was harshly put down by Chinese troops in 1959.

Since then, the Dalai Lama has been living in Dharamsala in northern India. As a political leader, he has peacefully campaigned for the freedom of Tibet; this has led to three United Nations resolutions on Tibet, in 1959, 1961, and 1965, respectively. In 1989, he received the Nobel Peace Prize for these efforts.

As a spiritual teacher, the Dalai Lama has travelled to and lectured in at least 67 countries and has written or co-written more than 110 books. In his speeches and writings, he has advocated peace, non-violence, inter-religious understanding, and universal responsibility. In *Beyond Religion: Ethics for a Whole World* (2011), he argues that in today's globalized world, no single religion, not even his own Buddhism, will be able to provide an ethical foundation that will be acceptable to all people. Instead, he proposes and explains a new, "secular" ethical framework.

Excerpts from His Holiness the Dalai Lama

Beyond Religion: Ethics for a Whole World
Chapter 1: Rethinking Secularism

© 2014 Cyril Hou. Used under license from Shutterstock, Inc.

Inner Values in an Age of Science

I am a man of religion, but religion alone cannot answer all our problems...

In light of our growing mastery over so many aspects of the physical world in the past two hundred years or so, it is not surprising that many people today question whether we have any need for religion at all. Things which in the

---

US Rights: Excerpts from BEYOND RELIGION: Ethics for a Whole World by His Holiness the Dalai Lama. Copyright © 2011 by His Holiness the Dalai Lama. Reprinted by permission of Houghton Mifflin Harcourt Publishing Company. All rights reserved. (pp. 3–6, 8–9, 11–17, 19, 103–112)

Canadian Rights: From BEYOND RELIGION: ETHICS FOR A WHOLE NEW WORLD by HIS HOLINESS THE DALAI LAMA. Copyright © 2011 by Aitken Alexander Associates, LLC. Reprinted by permission. (pp. 3–6, 8–9, 11–17, 19, 103–112)

past were only dreamt about—the elimination of diseases, space travel, computers—have become reality through science. So it is not surprising that many have come to place all their hopes in science, and even to believe that happiness can be achieved by means of what material science can deliver.

But while I can understand how science has undermined faith in some aspects of traditional religion, I see no reason why advances in science should have the same effect on the notion of inner or spiritual values. Indeed, the need for inner values is more pressing in this age of science than ever before.

In the attempt to make a compelling case for inner values and ethical living in an age of science, it would be ideal to make that case in wholly scientific terms. Although it is not yet possible to do so purely on the basis of scientific research, I am confident that as time goes on, a more and more secure scientific case for the benefits of inner ethical values will gradually emerge…

Fortunately, there is now a reasonably substantial body of evidence in evolutionary biology, neuroscience, and other fields suggesting that, even from the most rigorous scientific perspectives, unselfishness and concern for others are not only in our own interests but also, in a sense, innate to our biological nature. Such evidence, when combined with reflection on our personal experiences and coupled with simple common sense, can, I believe, offer a strong case for the benefits of cultivating basic human values that does not rely on religious principles or faith at all. And this I welcome.

Approaching Secularism

This then is the basis of what I call "secular ethics." I am aware that for some people, in particular for some Christian and Muslim brothers and sisters, my use of the word "secular" raises difficulties. To some, the very word suggests a firm rejection of, or even hostility toward, religion. It may seem to them that, in using this word, I am advocating the exclusion of religion from ethical systems, or even from all areas of public life. This is not at all what I have in mind. Instead, my understanding of the word "secular" comes from the way it is commonly used in India.

Modern India has a secular constitution and prides itself on being a secular country. In Indian usage, "secular," far from implying antagonism toward religion or toward people of faith, actually implies a profound respect for and tolerance toward all religions. It also implies an inclusive and impartial attitude which includes nonbelievers…

Secularism in India

For me, then, the word "secular" holds no fear. Instead, I am mindful of the founders of India's secular constitution, such as Dr. B.R. Ambedkar and Dr. Rajendra Prasad, the latter of whom I had the honor to know personally. Their intention in promoting secularism was not to do away with religion, but rather to recognize formally the religious diversity of Indian society. Mahatma Gandhi, the inspiration behind the constitution, was himself a deeply religious man. In his daily prayer meetings, he included readings and hymns from all the country's major faith traditions. This remarkable example is followed in Indian public ceremonies to this day.

The kind of religious tolerance Gandhi personified is nothing new in India. It has ancient roots, stretching back more than two thousand years. It is revealed, for example, on inscribed pillars dating from the reign of Emperor Ashoka in the third century BCE. One inscription contains the exhortation to "honor another's religion, for doing so strengthens both one's own and that of the other."

Tolerance in an Age of Globalization

Sometimes I describe myself as a modern-day messenger of ancient Indian thought. Two of the most important ideas I share wherever I travel—the principles of nonviolence and interreligious harmony—are both drawn from ancient Indian heritage. Though I am of course a Tibetan, I also consider myself to be, in a sense, a son of India. Since childhood my mind has been nourished by the classics of Indian thought. From the age of six, when I began my studies as a monk, the majority of the texts I read and memorized were by Indian Buddhist masters, many of whom were from the ancient university of Nalanda in central India. And since early adulthood my body, too, has been nourished by Indian fare: rice and *dal* (lentils).

So I am very happy to share and promote this Indian understanding of secularism, as I believe it can be of great value to all humanity. In today's interconnected and globalized world, it is not commonplace for people of dissimilar world views, faiths, and races to live side by side. I am often struck by this on my travels, especially in the West. For a considerable portion of humanity today, it is possible and indeed likely that one's neighbor, one's colleague, or one's employer will have a different mother tongue, eat different food, and follow a different religion than oneself.

It is a matter of great urgency, therefore, that we find ways to cooperate with one another in a spirit of mutual acceptance and respect. For while to many people it is a source of joy to live in a cosmopolitan environment where they can experience a wide spectrum of different cultures, there is no doubt that, for others, living in close proximity with those who do not share their language or culture can pose difficulties. It can create confusion, fear, and resentment, leading in the worst cases to open hostility and new ideologies of exclusion based on race, nationality, or religion. Unfortunately, as we look around the world, we see that social tensions are actually quite common. Furthermore, it seems likely that, as economic migration continues, such difficulties may even increase.

In such a world, I feel, it is vital for us to find a genuinely sustainable and universal approach to ethics, inner values, and personal integrity—an approach that can transcend religious, cultural, and racial differences and appeal to people at a fundamental human level. This search for a sustainable, universal approach is what I call the project of secular ethics.

Religion and Ethics

Though this book is not primarily about religion, in the interest of mutual understanding and respect between those with faith and those without it, I think it is worth spending a little time considering the relationship between religion and ethics.

For thousands of years, religion has been at the heart of human civilization. It is little wonder, then, that a concern for others and the basic inner values that emerge from this concern, such as kindness, honesty, patience, and forgiveness, have long been largely formulated in religious terms. In all of the world's major faith traditions, both theistic and non-theistic, these values, as well as those of self-discipline, contentment, and generosity, are celebrated as the keys to living a meaningful and worthwhile life. There is no surprise in this. Since religion's primary concern is with the human spirit, it is entirely natural that the practice of these inner values—which brings such rewards in terms of our own spiritual well-being and of those around us—should be integral to any religious practice.

The systems of belief with which the world's religions ground and support inner values can, generally speaking, be grouped into two categories.

On the one hand are the theistic religions, which include Hinduism, Sikhism, Zoroastrianism, Judaism, Christianity, and Islam. In these traditions, ethics is ultimately grounded in some understanding of God—as a creator and as the absolute ground of all that is. From a theistic point of view, the entire universe is part of a divine creation and plan, so the very fabric of that universe is sacred. And since God is infinite love or infinite compassion, loving others is part of loving and serving God. Also in many theistic traditions there is the belief that after death we will face divine judgment, and this provides a further strong incentive for behaving with restraint and due caution while here on Earth. When undertaken seriously, submission to God can have a powerful effect in reducing self-centeredness, and can thereby lay the foundation for a very secure ethical and even altruistic outlook.

On the other hand, in the non-theistic religions, such as Buddhism, Jainism, and a branch of the ancient Indian Samkhya school, there is no belief in a divine creator. Instead, there is the core principle of causality, while the universe is regarded as beginningless. Without a creator figure in which to ground inner values and an ethical life, the non-theistic religions instead ground ethics in the idea of karma. The Sanskrit word *karma* simply means "action." So when we talk about our karma, we are referring to all our intentional acts of body, speech, and mind, and when we talk about the *fruits* of our karma, we are talking about the consequences of these acts. The doctrine of karma is grounded in the observation of causality as a law of nature. Every intended action, word, or thought we have has a potentially unending stream of consequences. When combined with the idea of rebirth and successive lives, this understanding becomes a powerful basis for ethics and the cultivation of inner values. For example, a key Buddhist teaching on the cultivation of compassion involves, as part of establishing a deep empathetic connection with all beings, viewing all beings as having been one's mother at some stage in one's countless previous lives...

In the context of religion, these understandings—whether theistic or non-theistic—are of immense importance, since they provide the foundations not only for the determination to live ethically, but also for salvation or liberation itself. As such, for religious practitioners, the pursuit of an ethical life and their ultimate spiritual aspirations are inseparable.

I am not among those who think that humans will soon be ready to dispense with religion altogether. On the contrary, in my view, faith is a force for good and can be tremendously beneficial. In offering and understanding of human life which transcends our temporary physical existence, religion gives hope and strength to those facing adversity. The value of the world's great faith traditions is a subject I have discussed at some length in a previous book, *Toward a Kinship of Faiths*. For all its benefits, however—in bringing people together, giving guidance and solace, and offering a vision of the good life which people can strive to emulate—I do not think that religion is indispensable to the spiritual life.

But where does this leave us with regard to grounding ethics and nurturing inner values? Today, in a scientific age in which religion strikes many as meaningless, what basis for such values is left to us? How can we find a way to motivating ourselves ethically without recourse to traditional beliefs?

To my mind, although humans can manage without religion, they cannot manage without inner values. So my argument for the independence of ethics from religion is quite simple. As I see it, spirituality has two dimensions. The first dimension, that of basic spiritual well-being—by which I mean inner mental and emotional strength and balance—does not depend on religion but comes from our innate human nature as beings with a natural disposition toward compassion, kindness, and caring for others. The second dimension is what may be considered religion-based spirituality, which is acquired from our upbringing and culture and is tied to particular beliefs and practices. The difference between the two is something like the difference between water and tea. Ethics and inner values without religious content are like water, something we *need* every day for health and survival. Ethics and inner values based on a religious context are more like tea. The tea we drink is mostly composed of water, but it also contains some other ingredients—tea leaves, spices, perhaps some sugar or, at least in Tibet, salt—and this makes it more nutritious and sustaining and something we want every day. But however the tea is prepared, the primary ingredient is always water. While we can live without tea, we can't live without water. Likewise we are born free of religion, but we are not born free of the need for compassion...

Two Pillars for Secular Ethics

I believe that an inclusive approach to secular ethics, one with the potential to be universally accepted, requires recognition of only two basic principles. Both of these can easily be grasped on the basis of our common experience as humans and our common sense, and both are supported by findings of contemporary research, particularly in fields such as psychology, neuroscience, and the clinical sciences. The first principle is the recognition of our *shared humanity* and our shared aspiration to happiness and the avoidance of suffering; the second is the understanding of *interdependence* as a key feature of human reality, including our biological reality as social animals. From these two principles we can learn to appreciate the inextricable connection between our own well-being and that of others, and we can develop a genuine concern for others' welfare. Together, I believe, they constitute an adequate basis for establishing ethical awareness and the cultivation of inner values. It is through such values that we gain a sense of connection with others, and it is by moving beyond narrow self-interest that we find meaning, purpose, and satisfaction in life.

Study and Critical-Thinking Questions

1. a. In an age of science, why does the Dalai Lama believe religion is still needed? What does religion provide that science doesn't?
   b. On what issue do science and religion agree?
2. What does the Dalai Lama say he means by "secularism," drawing from its role in India? And what does he want to make sure the reader understands he does NOT mean by "secularism"?
3. What quote of Emperor Ashoka did the Dalai Lama mention? What do you think of this approach to other religions?
4. What does the Dalai Lama say are two of the most important ideas he shares wherever he travels?
5. What does he mean by "the project of secular ethics"?
6. List the values the Dalai Lama asserts are shared by all the major faith traditions.
7. The Dalai Lama discusses the foundation or grounding of ethics in theistic traditions and in non-theistic traditions.
   What does he say constitutes the foundation for ethics in the theistic traditions? In other words, how does belief lead to good or bad actions?

What constitutes the foundation for ethics in the non-theistic traditions? In other words, how does belief lead to good or bad actions?
8. What does the Dalai Lama say are the two pillars for secular ethics?

Chapter 8: Ethical Mindfulness in Everyday Life

Ethics is not simply a matter of knowing. More important, it is about doing. For this reason, even the most sophisticated ethical understanding, if it is not applied in daily life, is somewhat pointless. Living ethically requires not only the conscious adoption of an ethical outlook but also a commitment to developing and applying inner values in our daily lives.

Now, regarding the question of how to put ethics into practice in everyday life, it may be helpful to consider the process as having three aspects or levels—each progressively more advanced and dependent for its success upon the former. As outlined in some classical Buddhist texts, these are as follows: an ethic of restraint—deliberately refraining from doing actual or potential harm to others; an ethic of virtue—actively cultivating and enhancing our positive behavior and inner values; and an ethic of altruism—dedicating our lives, genuinely and selflessly, to the welfare of others.

To be effective, these three stages must be considered in relation to all our behavior. In other words, not just in relation to our outward physical actions, but also in relation to what we say, and ultimately to our very thoughts and intentions…

The Ethic of Restraint

Regarding certain kinds of obviously harmful behavior, all the world's major faiths and the humanistic traditions converge. Murder, theft, and inappropriate sexual conduct such as sexual exploitation are by definition harmful to others. So of course they should be abandoned.

But the ethic of restraint calls for more than this. Before we can contemplate actively benefiting others, we must first of all ensure that we do them no harm, even by our actions which are not immediately violent.

With regard to this principle of doing no harm, I am particularly impressed and humbled by my brothers and sisters in the Jain tradition. Jainism, which is something like a twin religion to Buddhism, places great emphasis on the virtue of nonviolence, or *ahimsa*, toward all beings. For example, Jain monks go to great lengths to ensure that they do not accidentally tread on insects or harm other living beings in their everyday activities.

However, the exemplary behavior of Jain monks and nuns is hard for all of us to emulate. Even for those whose circle of primary concern is restricted to humanity rather than encompassing all sentient beings, it can be very hard not to contribute to harming others through our actions in indirect ways. Consider, for example, how rivers come to be polluted: perhaps by mining companies extracting minerals, or industrial plants producing components that are crucial to the technologies we use on a daily basis. Every user of those technologies thereby is partly responsible for the pollution and thus contributes negatively to the lives of others. Unfortunately, it is perfectly possible to harm others indirectly through our actions without any intention of doing so.

So, realistically, I think the most important things we can all do to minimize the harm we inflict in our everyday lives is to apply discernment in our behavior, and to follow that natural sense of conscientiousness which arises from the enhanced awareness that discernment brings us.

Harm Caused by Nonviolent Means

While harm inflicted by outward actions can normally be seen, the suffering we inflict on others with words can be more hidden but is often no less damaging. This is particularly the case in our closest, most intimate relationships. We humans are quite sensitive, and it is easy to inflict suffering on those around us through our careless use of harsh words.

We can also inflict harm with dishonesty, slander, and divisive gossip. No doubt we have all, at some time or another, felt the negative consequences of such idle talk. It undermines trust and affection and can create all kinds of unfortunate misunderstandings and enmities between people. Here, as in other areas, we need to observe the "golden rule" found in all of the world's ethical systems: "Treat others as you would wish to be treated yourself" or "Do unto others as you would have them do unto you."

When it comes to avoiding harmful actions of body and speech, in addition to the fundamental rule, I personally find a list of six principles from a text by the second-century Indian Thinking Nagarjuna to be helpful. In this text, Nagarjuna is offering advice to an Indian monarch of the time. The six principles are as follows:

Avoid excessive use of intoxicants.
Uphold the principle of right livelihood.

Ensure that one's body, speech, and mind are nonviolent.

Treat others with respect.

Honor those worthy of esteem, such as parents, teachers, and those who are kind.

Be kind to others.

In spelling out what constitutes "right livelihood," Nagarjuna lists the following examples of a wrong approach to livelihood: trying to gain material benefits from others through pretense; using attractive words to gain things from others through deceit; praising another's possessions with the intention of trying to obtain them for oneself; forcibly taking what belongs to someone else; and extolling the qualities of what one has obtained in the past with the hope of receiving more.

Most of these pertain, in one form or another, to being dishonest. Dishonesty destroys the foundations of others' trust and is profoundly harmful. Transparency in our dealings with others is therefore tremendously important. Many of the scandals we hear about today, notably the corruption which is observable at so many levels and in so many fields—government, the judiciary, international finance, politics, media, even international sports—are related to this issue of right livelihood.

Heedfulness, Mindfulness, and Awareness

Just as a carpenter would not think of mending a chair without having a chisel, hammer, and saw near at hand, so too do we require a basic toolkit to help us in our daily effort to live ethically. In Buddhist tradition this toolkit is described in terms of three interrelated factors known as *heedfulness, mindfulness,* and *introspective awareness.* These three ideas may also be useful in a secular context. Together they can help us retain our core values in everyday life and guide our day-to-day behavior so that it becomes more in tune with the aim of bringing benefit to self and others.

The first of these, heedfulness, refers to adopting an overall stance of caution. The Tibetan term *bhakyo*, often translated as "heedfulness" or "conscientiousness," carries the sense of being careful and attentive. For example, if we are diagnosed as having diabetes, the doctor will advise us to be very careful with our diet. We must avoid sugar, salt, and fatty foods to keep our blood pressure and insulin in check. The doctor will warn us that if we fail to adhere to this dietary regime there may be serious consequences for our health. When patients care about their health, they will follow this advice and adopt an attitude of caution regarding their diet. When they are tempted to eat something they should avoid, this attitude or stance of caution will help them exercise restraint.

In one classical Buddhist text, heedfulness is illustrated with a story about a man convicted of a crime who is ordered by the king to carry a bowl of sesame oil, full to the brim, while a guard walks next to him carrying an unsheathed sword. The convict is warned that if he so much as spills a single drop of oil, he will be struck down with the sword. We can imagine how careful and vigilant the convict would be! He would have complete presence of mind and total attentiveness. The story illustrates how closely related heedfulness is to the qualities of mindfulness and awareness described below...

Today there are many secularized techniques for the development of mindfulness, and these have been shown to be effective in stress reduction and the treatment of depression. As I understand it, mindfulness in this context usually refers to gaining awareness of our own patterns of behavior, including thoughts and feelings, and learning to let go of those habits, thoughts, and emotions which are unhelpful. This seems a very worthwhile endeavor. . . .

Yet, in the context of living ethically on a day-to-day basis, in my view the most important meaning of mindfulness is *recollection*. In other words, mindfulness is the ability to gather oneself mentally and thereby recall one's core values and motivation. In Tibetan the word for mindfulness, *drenpa*, also means "memory," so it suggests bringing presence of mind into everyday activities. With such recollection, we are less likely to indulge our bad habits and more likely to refrain from harmful deeds. Littering, being wasteful, and overindulging oneself are all simple examples of behavior which can be improved through the application of mindfulness.

Awareness, or *sheshin* in Tibetan, means paying attention to our own behavior. It means honestly observing our behavior as it is going on, and thereby bringing it under control. By being aware of our words and actions, we guard ourselves against doing and saying things we will later regret. When we are angry, for instance, and if we fail to recognize that our anger is distorting our perception, we may say things we do not mean. So having the ability to monitor oneself, having, as it were, a second order level of attention is of great practical use in everyday life, as it gives us greater control over our negative behavior and enables us to remain true to our deeper motives and convictions.

Such awareness of our own behavior—our actions, thoughts, and words—is not something we can learn overnight. Rather, it develops gradually, and we become more aware, we slowly gain mastery…

Practicing awareness is not quite the same as listening to your conscience, however. In Buddhist ethical theory there is no idea of the conscience as a distinct mental faculty. But being conscientious is still very important. It is described in terms of two key mental qualities, namely *self-respect* and *consideration of others.*

The first of these, self-respect, relates to having a sense of personal integrity, a self-image as a person who upholds certain values. So when we are tempted to indulge in harmful behavior, our self-image acts as a restraint, as we think "this is unbecoming of me." The second mental quality, consideration of others, pertains to having a healthy regard for others' opinions, especially for their potential disapproval. Together, these two factors give us an added level of caution about doing wrong which can strengthen our moral compass.

The Ethic of Virtue

If, through mindfulness, awareness, and heedfulness, we can manage to refrain from harming others in our everyday actions and words, we can start to give more serious attention to actively doing good, and this can be a source of great joy and inner confidence. We can benefit others through our actions by being warm and generous toward them, by being charitable, and by helping those in need. Therefore, when misfortune befalls others, or they make mistakes, rather than responding with ridicule or blame, we must reach out and help them. Benefiting others through our speech includes praising others, listening to their problem, and offering them advice and encouragement.

To help us bring benefit to others through our words and actions, it is useful to cultivate an attitude of sympathetic joy in others' achievements and good fortune. This attitude is a powerful antidote against envy, which is not only a source of unnecessary suffering on the individual level but also an obstacle to our ability to reach out and engage with others. Tibetan teachers often say that such sympathetic joy is the least costly way of promoting one's own virtues.

The Ethic of Altruism

Altruism is a genuinely selfless dedication of one's actions and words to the benefit of others. All the world's religious traditions recognize this as the highest form of ethical practice, and in many it is seen as the main avenue to liberation or to unity with God.

But though a complete and selfless dedication to others is the highest form of ethical practice, this does not mean that altruism cannot be undertaken by anyone. In fact many people in caring professions such as social work and health care, and also those in teaching, are involved in the pursuit of this third level of ethics. Such professions, which bring direct benefit to the lives of so many, are truly noble. Yet there are countless other ways in which ordinary people can and do lead lives which benefit others. What is required is simply that we make serving others a priority.

An important part of serving others is using discernment to assess the likely consequences of our own actions. Then, by being heedful, mindful, and attentive in our everyday lives, we will begin to gain mastery over our actions and worlds. This is the very foundation of freedom, and it is through gaining such self-mastery, using it to ensure that our actions are non-harmful at every level, that we can start to actively work for the benefit of others.

Study and Critical-Thinking Questions

1. The Dalai Lama starts out saying that ethics is about *both* _____ and _____.
2. List and briefly explain the three aspects or levels of putting ethics into practice in daily life.
3. The Dalai Lama asserts that these aspects are not only confined to our actions, but also ...
4. In discussing the ethics of restraint, the Dalai Lama describes this as "doing no _____."
   What kinds of behaviors does he discuss in this and the next section (Harm Caused by non-Violent Means) that could bring harm—thus, one should restrain from?

5. What three tools does the Dalai Lama say are needed in order to live ethically? Briefly describe what he means by each.
6. What is the Ethic of Virtue?
7. What is the Ethic of Altruism?
8. What is one point the Dalai Lama makes in this chapter that you find useful in your own thinking about yourself as an ethical leader? Please give an example of a potential situation in which one of the Dalai Lama's principles or ideas might guide you.

© 2014 Galyna Andrushko. Used under license from Shutterstock, Inc.